Affiliate Mar

Step By Step Guide To Make $10,000/Month Passive Income To Escape The Rat Race and Build an Successful Digital Business From Home

Table of Contents

Introduction

The ultimate career aim for many people is to earn a passive income. A passive income needs little to no effort, allowing you to pursue a variety of exciting alternatives, such as early retirement or the flexibility to live your life as you like without the constraints of a traditional nine-to-five job.

Most of us would gladly accept the opportunity to earn a passive income and forgo working eight hours a day, five days a week. Do you want to be 20-30 years ahead of your friends and family when it comes to retirement? Maybe you'd like to be able to travel the world at your leisure and fly away anytime you desire. In either case, a passive income is essential to living the life you've always desired.

But how does one go about earning money in this manner? For many people, it appears to be nothing more than a pleasant fantasy. However, this need not be the case. If you want to start living the life you've only dreamed about, you might be surprised to learn that it's closer than you think. As online shopping grows in popularity throughout the world, affiliate marketing is becoming the path of choice for consumers seeking a passive income. Affiliate marketing allows regular people to build home-based companies and generate a passive income by promoting and selling other people's products, which is becoming more common as more businesses provide their products and services online.

1. What Is Affiliate Marketing?

Broadly speaking, whoever is on the other side of the equation from you, as the affiliate marketer is referred to as the merchant, and they all need the help from affiliate marketers like you to get their product out to the masses? This need is met by the affiliate marketer, also known as the publisher, who can be a single individual looking to generate a passive income, or a large company devoted to doing the same thing on a much larger scale. This marketing can be done via a variety of different means, though the most common of which is by reviewing specific products, often those targeted at a specific group or niche. These reviews are then cataloged on a website that is specifically targeted at the portion of the audience who are most likely to make a purchase.

It is essential to check the type of support that the program provides. You must have customer care service numbers that you can call in case you have any queries and have quick solutions to problems.

Site Building

Once you identify your niche market and research your affiliates, you can build your site. This step is all about putting your plans into action. If you already have a website or a blog up and running, then you must work on finding your affiliates. But if you don't have one, then here are the steps to adopt.

First off, you have to decide upon a domain name and pick something that is unique to you. You must be recognizable so that people know it's your website. Many popular websites give you the chance to register your domain name, such as GoDaddy.com. Once you decide on the title, check if it is available and buy it so that you don't lose the chance of getting your desired domain name.

Once done, you have to set up the blog or website. Look for reliable hosts who give you good features to work with. Some good hosts include Blue Host and GoDaddy.com.

Next, you have to install Word Press so that you have a CMS to work with. You will be given a one-click option that you can use to install it on your site.

Next, you have to install the theme and make it unique.

Once done, you have to add the content. It is this content that will help you find your target affiliates.

Making the Content

One of the most critical steps involved in the process of affiliate marketing is creating content. The content is what draws people to your blog or website and helps with finding affiliates. Remember that content is King, and it is essential to come up with some that brings value to your customer. If you need help in knowing some of the lucrative niches, then they are as follows:

Reviews

Everybody loves seeing reviews and reactions. If you wish to create a niche for yourself, then you must review products that have not yet been reviewed or be the first one to review something. You can choose any niche you like such as makeup, technology, kitchen appliances, etc. In doing so, you get the opportunity of having these sent over to you to review them.

Blogs on Current Affairs
Remember that the Internet is one of the best tools to use to find information. More and more people use the Internet to find relevant information. If you give them that information, then you can instantly catapult your popularity. People will keep coming back to your blog if they keep getting the latest news and updates. For example, if you keep updating your blog about the latest fashion trends or news about stocks, then people will keep coming back to your blog for the latest information.

Free Courses
People tend to look for places where they can get free content. This can be an eBook, dance lessons, singing lessons, language lessons, make up instructions, etc. All these happen to be niche ideas that you can use to find your target audience. You can make use of email marketing to generate leads and get more and more people to view your videos or visit your blog page. A good way of monetizing it is by incorporating the products that you wish to sell so that you can promote it effortlessly. You have to know that nobody will be interested in generic content and need something specific. Generic content leads to lesser traffic, and in turn lower sales. So, you have to put in the effort of giving them value-based products that are sure to keep them coming back for more.

Building an Audience
The next task for you is to build a large audience base. The audience is what will help you get your affiliate marketing rolling. Many people assume that an audience will start building as soon as you get your blog rolling. But this is not true, as you have to put in the effort of finding an audience and retaining them. Remember that you will require a steady stream of views to maintain popularity. For this, you have to do certain things that will keep your audience interested in what you are putting out. Here are some tips to help you increase your customer base.

Social Media
Social media is all about assisting people to promote their business and grab as many eyeballs as possible. If you are not making use of social media to promote your blogs and

websites, then you are missing out on almost 50% more audience. There are many different social media platforms to choose from, including Facebook, Twitter, and Instagram. You have to link all of them together so that you can make the most of their promotional capabilities. Create a Facebook page and share it with your contacts. You can ask your friends to share too so that you can increase your viewership. Link all your social media accounts so that people know you are the same person and have an online business.

Collaborations

It is essential to collaborate with others so that you can promote your channel. If there is someone who has a lot more subscribers and followers than you, then you can ask them to be a guest on your blog, in your videos or feature in theirs. You might have to pay them an incentive for it, but it will be well worth it as you can increase your viewership. If you happen to capitalize on even 40% of their audience, then you will successfully increase your audience base. Do as much collaboration as you can so that you can increase your chances of finding a bigger audience.

Power of SEO
SEO stands for search engine optimization and using it the right way can help you increase your audience base by a large margin. When you wish to make use of search engine optimization, you have to ensure that you know what words and hashtags to use so that you can reach out to a large audience. You can make use of a tool that will give you these words that can be used to catapult your popularity and be noticed more.

Email Lists
Email marketing can help you promote your blog, website, or channel by sending regular updates. You increase chances of people clicking on your blog link if you keep sending them reminders. Remember that you have to time the emails so that they reach the audience at the right times. Early evenings are the best time to send reminders.

Paid Advertising
Some affiliate marketers engage in paid advertising to increase their traffic and drive up product sales. Paid advertising can be done through social media, as it is easier to do so. Google Ad Words is a good tool to drive sales and traffic up.

Promoting Affiliates
This happens to be the most crucial part of the monetizing process. Once your blog, website or channel is on a roll, you must promote your affiliate's products and services. The basic idea is to sell to as many people as possible so that you can increase sales. Here are some ways in which you can promote affiliate products.

Product Reviews

One of the best ways to promote products is through product reviews. Your affiliate merchant will send products that you have to review for them. You have to add in links to the product so that those who like it can be led to the website to purchase the product. Remember that honest reviews are much better than fabricated ones. You have to build your credibility by telling people your real experiences and what they can expect from the product. Once you add the link and your audience member buys the product, then you have made your first sale!

Ads

Banner ads have been around for a long time and are one of the most popular ways of advertising products. Affiliate marketers post banner ads on their blogs and websites so that people can click on it and be redirected to the product website. All that you have to do is place the ad on a page that has lots of traffic. This will increase your sales. You have to find the best page to place the banners to capitalize on this technique.

Context Links

Context links are some of the easiest ways of promoting products and services belonging to affiliates. It is where you add the links to certain aspects of your blog, such as specific words that will lead the audience to the product. For example, if you run a food-based blog then you can link ingredients to actual products that you used to prepare the recipe. Your audience will be interested in using the same ingredients and will most likely click on the link to buy. This will help you increase sales and, in turn, your income.

Email Promotion

As mentioned earlier, using email is still a very lucrative way of capitalizing on your audience base. You can use the leads to send them product links and links to reviews. They can click on it and be redirected to the products. If you have a large following, then merely clicking on the link can help you monetize your affiliate links.

Discounts and Giveaways

Everybody loves discounts! One of the best ways to promote affiliate products is by offering your audience a unique discount that they can only get through your blog, website, or channel. You can also inform your audience about a sale that is currently running on the website. Giveaways are also a big hit. You can give away products to a lucky winner, etc.

These are the different ways in which you can promote products and it's best to choose a technique that works well. Remember that some affiliates will have rigid rules for ways in which you can promote their products. Some will only accept banner ads, while others will only accept email marketing, etc. You have to use the same to stay within promotional parameters.

Bear in mind that it is now mandatory, as per US FTC laws, to put up a disclaimer on your website or blog that says you have affiliate links with the company whose products you are promoting. This will work as a basic courtesy towards your viewers so that they know about it when they click on the links.

Repeat

The last step of the process is repeating all the above steps. You have to adopt the same measures for all the new businesses that you set up. It is important to continue what you are doing so that your audience base can be consistently expanded, and you have more businesses to fall back on.

2.   Profitable Affiliate Marketing Niches

What exactly is a niche?

A niche is a specific topic about which you will blog or a narrow subject if you choose. It means you focus your blog on a small number of topics rather than writing and publishing blogs on everything. This is beneficial since it informs people about your site and why they should subscribe.

Why did you decide on a specific niche?

Several reasons why focusing on a specific specialty is a good idea.

Some people, for example, wonder if it makes sense to write content on their blog about meditation and cryptocurrencies if both categories are beneficial in terms of affiliate earnings.

The issue with such diversity on a blog might make readers feel they've landed on the wrong one.

Consider what to put on your site to clarify that you're talking about fashion and motorcycles. Of course, you might find them both fascinating, but most of your readers will not. It is preferable to select one of the two blog niches or create two separate blog websites.

As I've previously stated on my blog, it's easier to make $100 from ten affiliate marketing websites than make $1000 from one.

Google's free visitors and marketing specialties

Google is another crucial factor to consider while deciding on a niche.

Most of your traffic will come from Google's free visitors if you want to make money blogging.

For example, your blog will rank high in the search results, bringing many "free" visitors to your website each month, allowing you to earn money.

If you build your niche website laser-sharp on the issue, visitors from Google are not only "free," but they are also highly targeted and will be interested in all of the associated things you give them.

It's easier to get this kind of organic traffic when your website's purpose is obvious (to you, Google, and your visitors).

So pick a niche and concentrate solely on it. Read our affiliate marketing tutorials on how to target a tiny niche:

What are the considerations you must make?

If you want to generate money with affiliate marketing, picking a specialty is a long-term decision. Especially if you want to grow your blog and generate a lot of money (some people make $100,000 per month), choose a niche that you are truly passionate about so that you can create blog posts even when you are not feeling inspired.

What factors should you consider while building a micro-niche affiliate marketing campaign?

You must respond 'YES' to the following three questions:

• Do you have a strong interest in this field?

• Are there others who share your enthusiasm for that niche?

• Is there enough money in your specialty to go around?

If that's the case, you're good to go.

A happy, excited woman smiles broadly - You're ready to embark on your affiliate marketing adventure.

Then you'll be able to confidently choose a niche. Look through the list below to find one of the 100+ niches profitable in the affiliate marketing industry.

AFFILIATE MARKETING'S TOP 100 NICHES

Are you looking for blog niche ideas for the year 2023? We've got you covered. You can use this list of profitable niches to start a business in 2023 or improve an existing one. There are over 100 niche ideas organized into categories to help you get started with your new affiliate website:

Affiliate marketing specializations in health and sports

By 2020, it is estimated to reach $3.31 trillion. People are beginning to take action because they are concerned about their health due to the coronavirus outbreak.

Health and wellness encompass the mind, body, and soul. Sub-niches include personal care, nutrition, preventative medicine, and alternative medicine by purchasing a gluten-free product at the grocery store.

- *Weightlifting*
- *Yoga*
- *Jogging*
- *Meditation*
- Fitness sports
- *E-sports*
- *Hiking*
- Mental health
- *Psychology*
- Alternative medicines
- Natural medicines
- *Massages*
- *Skincare*
- Aging / Anti-aging
- Lose weight
- Muscle growth
- Exercise at home

Lifestyle affiliate marketing niches

- *Pregnancy*
- *Traveling*
- Digital nomads
- Van life
- Tiny houses
- Dating / online dating
- *Marriage*
- *Separation*
- *Education*
- *Self-study*
- Ecological products
- Sustainable living
- *Education*

Hobbies affiliate marketing niches

- *Cars*
- *Engines*
- *Gaming*

- *Technology*
- *Gadgets*
- *Music*
- *Gardening*
- *Photography*
- *Videography*
- *Fishing*
- *Survivors*

Do it yourself/ DIY

- Painting and art
- *Movies*
- Poker and gambling
- *Writing*
- *Drones*
- *Books*
- *Cameras*
- Virtual reality
- *Computers*

Food blog affiliate marketing niches

- *Recipes*
- *Veganism*
- Vegetarian food
- Cooking advice
- *Baking*
- *Diets*
- *Cakes*
- Home brewery
- *Beer*
- *Liqueurs*
- *Wine*
- Kitchen supplements
- *Cookware*
- National dishes

Finances affiliate marketing niches

- Personal finances

To invest

- *Cryptocurrencies*
- *Shares*

- Stock market
- Housing market
- Financial independence
Passive income

- Local businesses
- Career Advice
- *Freelancing*
- Doing business online
- *Retire*
- Budget lifestyle
-

Affiliate marketing niches in fashion and beauty

Covering trending subjects in the fashion business will help you get a lot of traffic from search engines. Creating a successful blog that follows trends or offers online courses with a stylist might be difficult since you must continuously stay current. However, there is a vast array of affiliate product ideas, most of which have large search traffic in SERPs. Covering hot issues in this category can help you access a multibillion-dollar market.

- Nail stylist
- *Makeup*
- Personal style
- Fashion clothing
- *Haircare*
- Celebrities / gossip
- *Tattoos*
- *Watches*

Affiliate marketing areas for personal development

This is a significant web niche, commonly known as self-help. There are books, videos, online training, and coaching accessible, as well as courses and programs. There is a self-improvement product for everyone who wants to boost their self-esteem, attain professional success, boost their confidence, set and achieve goals, and conquer obstacles.

Tony Robbins is a name you've probably heard of. The same thing. It's a huge industry that's always growing. People want to be happy, content in their life, and worry-free. They also rarely buy a single book or program, which favors recurrent purchases and higher-ticket items in this market.

You don't need to be a famous name like Tony Robbins or Jack Canfield, nor do you need to have a well-known brand like The Secret. A very profitable internet business may be built on a little fraction of this vast market.

- *Self-development*
- *Productivity*
- Time management
- Get rid of bad habits
- Quit smoking
- Stop drinking
- Relationship advice
- Learning a language
- Learning to play an instrument
- *Motivational*
- Healthy habits
- Breathwork / Wim Hof

Although this is not an exhaustive list of personal development niches, these are the best-paying and most popular personal development niches to promote right now.

Making money online and marketing

- Social media
- Digital freelancing
- *SEO*
- Graphic design
- *E-commerce*
- *E-shops*
- *Shopify*
- *WordPress*
- *Wix*
- Affiliate Marketing
- Content marketing
- *Blogging*
- *Encoding*
- Mobile apps
- *Self-publishing*
- Youtube (learn more about YouTube affiliate Marketing)
- Affiliate marketing software
- Advertise online
- Performance marketing software

- *Google*

Affiliate Marketing Niche for Pet Owners

The pet sector in the United States is expected to generate $99 billion in expenditures by 2020. As a result, it's safe to assume that pets are a lucrative niche. Different types of pets, lifestyles, and other factors can help you carve out a niche in this business.

While most people own fish, dogs, or cats, there are a variety of other strange pets available, including horses, lizards, turtles, and even chickens, each with its own set of advantages. Of course, there are more niches to consider, but these are the most basic:

- Traveling with pets
- Collars by designers
- food for pets
- canine education

Now, let's look at some of the most often asked questions about affiliate marketing niches.

What are the most promising niches for the year 2023?

In 2023, you can use the complete list above to find a profitable affiliate marketing niche for your company. However, goods relevant to the recent Coronavirus outbreak, such as face masks, hand sanitizers, and disinfection sprays, are included in some 2021 niches.

In 2023, what products will be popular?

Home exercise equipment, natural care items, pet products, keto supplements, and natural oils are among the top trending and most popular E-commerce themes for 2023.

What will be the most popular item on Amazon in 2023?

Alexa TV remote, Alexa Echo Dot Smart Speaker, Fujifilm INSTAX Mini Film, Fujifilm Instax Camera, Instant Pot, PlayStation, and Nintendo gift cards and games were the most popular items in 2020.

How do you pick an affiliate marketing niche?

I usually recommend picking a niche industry in which you are interested and knowledgeable, so you can have fun developing content and discovering goods to advertise along the road. If you are not sure how to choose an affiliate marketing niche, look at the list above and attempt to choose something that interests you.

Is it advantageous to work in the travel affiliate marketing niche?

It's a big old globe out there, and owing to a plethora of low-cost airlines, even the most isolated areas may be explored without winning the lottery. Okay, you'll have to fly economy class instead of business class, but that's a tiny price to pay for the convenience.

More people are moving now than at any other time in human history. For countries concerned about pandemics, this is bad news. But it's wonderful news for the travel sector, which is predicted to generate $7 trillion in revenue every year (yep, with a "t").

That means it's one of the most profitable affiliate categories, with plenty of lucrative schemes to get you started. Furthermore, travel spans a vast range of niches and sub-niches, including anything from typical hotels and flights to city guides, luggage, insurance, and even clothing. You can sell them as a digital download.

However, you do not need to take the same hasty strategy as other affiliates, namely, flinging inexpensive flights and rooms.

How do you make money as a home security affiliate?

I had never considered home security as an affiliate marketing topic until lately. Everything changed when my house was broken into more than two years ago. By the way, having your home broken into is a horrible experience.

I made home security a major priority because my girlfriend was afraid to sleep at night.

My locks, window security latches, Wi-Fi cameras, motion sensor lights on the outside, and a controlled home alarm system with several interior sensors were all improved. In short, I spent about a thousand dollars to re-establish her sense of security.

And one of the features that identify strong niches for affiliate marketing is a sense of urgency. Every year, 1.24 million houses in the United States are broken into, so you're dealing with a highly targeted market that needs your help.

Is the ketogenic diet a lucrative affiliate marketing niche in 2023?

If you are not familiar with the Keto diet, it's simply low carbohydrate nutrition disguised as something else. The keto diet's success, on the other hand, stems from the fact that those who follow it lose a lot of weight in a short length of time.

Thirty pounds in a month, for example. Like any other type of diet, Keto eating has a vast potential audience and a fervent following. Existing Keto devotees are still looking for the latest snack or supplement to add to their diet. This is where affiliate products like yours come in helpful.

Many new people to Keto are looking for a fun way to get started and the right steps to take. You need to put the correct products in front of Keto dieters, and they'll buy them straight away.

That's all we could come up with regarding affiliate marketing website niche market suggestions. Best of luck in making money from it!

3.   Driving Free Traffic

Many people have the mistaken belief that the days of free traffic ended long ago, and worrying about things like SEO is a waste of time. Or they mistakenly believe that Facebook advertising is the gift of the ages and it's all you need. The fact is they are wrong on all counts. Think about Facebook – they are under a lot of scrutiny and prices are rising due to increased competition. Facebook users are also getting concerned about being manipulated by marketers, so it's not as easy as it was three or five years ago to show them an ad and get them signing up for your list or even buying products. So you don't want to be dependent on paid advertising, and we are talking about FREE traffic here, so why not take advantage of it?

In this chapter, we are going to give you an overview of a reliable process that can help you drive free traffic to your offers. Admittedly, this is not something that people looking to earn money fast are going to be happy with because it does involve a lot of upfront work and it takes time to start driving traffic to your site. But once it starts working, it can be like a snowball rolling downhill, gradually picking up momentum. Once it's going you will be generating long-term traffic that keeps coming without having to put more work in, and it can grow and grow if you keep up with the efforts, leading to more sales and higher levels of income.

With free traffic, it begins with blogging.

A blog to Target Keywords

The first step that you need to take care of is making sure that your blog looks good. While you can install WordPress and use a free template, the free templates don't look as good or as professional and that is going to hurt you in the long run. Invest the $45 to get a good template that you can use to make your blog visually appealing. Remember that in the affiliate marketing business information is king, so this is important.

Next, you are going to want to sign up for a service called Yoast. It's a plug-in that you install on your word press blog. While Yoast has a paid subscription you can get, they offer free tools and those are all 95% of people are going to need. Yoast will analyze your posts and help you optimize them. You will want to use its suggestions and incorporate them in your writing, and also use its capability to set up the headline and text that will show up in Google search for each individual blog post.

The next step is to follow a specific writing style. Each post you put up should have 2-3 images in the post. Break up text into chunks that are separated by h2 headlines and images. This not only helps make your blog more readable, but it's going to make Google look upon it more favorably. You can also help make your blog appealing by incorporating (via embed) related YouTube videos.

Don't put very many external links. What you don't want is people coming to visit your blog and then clicking off to go somewhere else. Instead, write a set of related posts on your blog, and then the link between them. Interlinking also helps drive traffic. As your blog develops, as random traffic comes to different blog posts, the links between them will help keep people on your site longer as they click through to read different articles.

Of course, you can incorporate your affiliate links to the products you are promoting. This can be done either implicitly, which means you link to the product in the text as a part of the conversation, or you explicitly in a product review or recommendation.

The focus of each blog post should be writing about real information on the niche, and not about doing hard selling.

Incorporating SEO

You don't have to be an SEO expert to benefit from it. Earlier in the book, we already gave you the first steps. Do your keyword research, and then compile a list of keywords. Each keyword (focus on long phrase ones) is then the anchor word for an article. It can be the basis of the topic of individual articles or part of the basis for it. For example, "keto diet food list" is one idea, and "cheap foods for the keto diet" would be another. Whatever niche you select, you can find many phrases like that which can easily be turned into articles.

Google loves content and it loves substantial content. Therefore you should avoid cutting corners by having blog posts that are short. Make your posts between 800-1,500 words in length. They don't have to be super long, and you don't want to bore readers either – but you want readers and Google to see the site as one that is an information-packed authority site.

So you are going to want to use the keyword or keyword phrase for the article title and in one subtitle. Then have the phrase appear two to three times within the article itself. It can also help if one of your links is the keyword phrase or has it in it.

Make sure the "slug" which is the link created for the blog post includes the key phrase in it as well.

That is really all you need to know about SEO. You don't need to take an expensive class or do anything more than what we've described here.

-

Post Regularly

The bottom line is that you are starting a business, so you should not be afraid of putting some work in. That doesn't mean you have to work at it 60 hours a week. But the bottom line is the more blog posts you write, the more traffic you are going to be getting. And the more frequently that you post, the faster you're going to generate free traffic.

We recommend that you post at a minimum three times per week, and up to once per day. This pattern looks natural to Google. Unnatural patterns, like paying people on Fiverr or something to write hundreds of posts for you and then putting them up all at once, looks fake and Google might actually penalize the site. Make it look like its real, genuine content that follows a natural posting pattern that someone genuinely interested in the niche would use. That guarantees long term success; again trying to cut corners does not and may even hurt you.

However, make sure each post is valid. Don't post about posting, post about topics that you've gotten from your keyword list. If you don't have time to write a valid and thorough post on one day, take a day off to make sure you get it right and don't post for the sake of posting. Remember to be patient, this is a long term process.

Collect Emails

You are going to want to collect the email addresses of people that visit your blog, and then sell to them using your email autoresponder. We aren't going to review the technical details of setting that up, but you want a popup that shows up when people click on the site, offering them something free in exchange for signing up with their email address. Many vendors on ClickBank or elsewhere offer free books or video courses that you can give away to people interested in the niche. Alternatively, you can write your own, and in this one instance, it might be something that you can hire outside help to create. But make sure its good quality, remember you want your prospects to associate you with good, reliable information so that when you recommend products they are likely to take your recommendation.

Create backlinks

After you have a few posts on your blog, you are going to want to start posting links to specific articles when relevant. This can be done on forums related to your niche or on websites like Quora. To avoid being banned, make sure there is some relevance to posting the link on the site. Also, do it as an afterthought and make sure you are participating in the form or on Quora and posting real responses to people's questions and commentary. Always remember the keyword is content! Posting backlinks to posts on your blog is going to help your blog get ranked higher on the search engines.

Robots and Crawling

After you set up your blog, be sure to submit the site to Google webmaster tools and Bing. While they supposedly automatically crawl the entire internet and so find things on their own, there is no sense in waiting and you are going to want to put yourself forward and submit it manually to speed things along. Also, check your robots.txt file. This is beyond the scope of the book, but you can look it up online and search for situations when robots.txt is keeping your site from being indexed. Make sure that is not happening in your case.

YouTube Channel

Having a YouTube channel for your niche is an important way to drive more traffic. It might not be essential, but with two affiliate marketers, if one has a blog but the other has a blog and a YouTube channel, the latter marketer is going to close a lot more sales.

You can make simple videos talking about your niche. You can even just summarize what you are talking about in your blog posts. It doesn't have to be a fancy video promotion; some of the most popular YouTube channels are those that have people simply talking on camera with self-recorded videos. You can even just use your smartphone to make and post the videos.

You aren't shooting for becoming a star, you are just looking for another way to provide good information to people and drive traffic. So the videos don't have to be perfect. Don't be camera shy, it's not that important. Being perfect or looking perfect isn't the goal here. When it comes to marketing a genuine presentation is going to go far. And something that seems like a regular person giving real information is worth more than gold.

A tool you should be aware of is VidIQ. It's free and you can install it in your browser, and find out what tags people are using on their videos that are related to yours.

In addition, we are going to want to use our YouTube videos to create more backlinks to the blog. That's why it's a good idea to connect the topics of your videos two topics of your blog posts. Then under each video in the description for the link back towards the blog. You can also do video reviews of affiliate products and put links including your affiliate link underneath your video descriptions. However, it's essential to make your reviews as authentic as possible. A good video review of an affiliate product can be extremely effective. There is nothing more successful than having a video of a person giving an authentic description of a product without using a hard selling technique, but giving the people the ability to link into the product and purchase it. So in that sense our YouTube channel we will have dual purposes. It will help put some backlinks to the blog to help bring those up in searches, and I will also help drive some traffic directly to the affiliate offers.

Using Your Facebook Page

A Facebook page is also an important part of your marketing. This can also be another tool that you can use to set up some backlinks that go back to the blog. One of the nice things about Facebook is that they allow you to create Facebook pages that are not connected directly to your personal profile. That information is kept a secret from your Facebook friends and personal connections. You can reveal it if you choose to but the idea here is that you can create Facebook pages that are often associated with the business, or even with pen names and personalities that you used to market products.

So in this context of trying to drive free traffic, one of the things that you will want to utilize is the ability to Post on the blog and then put a link back to the blog from the Facebook page. You can share the Facebook page on your blog. Later, if you do advertising on Facebook you can start to build up a Fanbase for the Facebook page. Now if you're going to do free traffic or rely entirely on advertising, it can help to have a Facebook page that has at least some content associated with it. So that's why we recommend that you start a blog and you have backlinks back and forth between the two. That way when people go to see your Facebook page there is going to be a wealth of information already on the page. Moreover, if you're posting good and useful content that can help get people curious and they may go back and check out your blog and sign-up for your email newsletters.

Landing Page

In most cases, your landing page is going to be part of paid advertising campaigns. That said, you can also utilize it when driving free traffic. So no matter what you're going to do you should get one set up. I encourage readers to do some research online to find out how to make an effective landing page. We can't go into the details here because there's not enough space. But basically, you're landing page needs to have a professional and clean appearance, with a good-looking photograph and a headline with some effective copy.

As we stated earlier, we believe that click funnels are by far the best tool that can be used to create landing pages. In fact, click funnels lets you do a lot more than that but that's that you can find out when checking it out for yourself. The important thing is to have a landing page ready before you go on and do things like start posting a lot to Instagram. You can also try to drive traffic from your Facebook page to the landing page. So the only purpose of the landing page is really to collect emails and then we are going to run email marketing campaigns to the people that sign-up on the email list.

Instagram

The next topic we're going to discuss is one platform that is often ignored. Instagram is a very powerful social media platform that you can use to promote your affiliate offers and drive a lot of traffic much of free traffic. For those who are not familiar with it let's describe what it is in a nutshell.

First of all, you need to understand that this isn't a website per se. Instagram is almost entirely a mobile application. So to create an account if you don't have one, you are going to want to download the app onto your mobile phone. Even if you already have an account, you are going to want to create a new one.

Instagram has three account types. The first is obviously a personal account. You don't want to be using your personal account to promote affiliate offers. For one thing, it's going to turn off your friends. Also, it's going to create confusion if you are using it to promote affiliate offers that belong to one niche or another.

They also allow the creation of a business account. This could be useful if you're going to be focused completely on one area. However, they also allow the creation of a niche account and for most affiliate marketers that are going to be the most suitable way to set things up. So keep in mind that you may want to have multiple Instagram accounts. You can have one for each one of your niches.

So where do you go from here? It's going to be like running a blog except this is going to be a visual blog. If you aren't familiar with what the app is it's basically an image sharing app. But you're going to make your images marketing images. So it will include a picture along with an important message that could be used to promote a product that you were using for your affiliate business. Recently, or maybe it's not that recently in social media time, Instagram also allows people to post short videos that are called stories. They are not very long, it's probably 15 seconds maximum. Even so, remember that for decades advertisers have been pushing products on television using 30-second spots. So that doesn't mean you can't do some very effective marketing with this tool.

To get started, you're going to want to start posting some nice images with text on them along with some occasional story videos. You can look in the app store and find Apps that are specially designed for use with Instagram. You don't have to use those but it's helpful to have some really nice text overlays without having to resort to using Photoshop or something like that.

Basically, you're going to treat this as if it was a blog. So you want to be putting up stuff aka content on your Instagram account, at least three days a week. Again, the more the better. You are also going to want to find other people on Instagram that are interested in the same niche. In fact, you might want to use this for spying purposes in the beginning so that you can get an idea of how to post effectively. But what you want to do is you want to start following people. The idea is to encourage them to follow you which some of them will.

Now, unfortunately, this is not something that's going to pay off overnight. It's probably going to take a few months just like blogging is. But in the end, it's going to be worth it.

Once again, this is going to work with a snowball effect and eventually, you're going to find that if you stick with it it's going to generate a lot of followers for you. But we are doing this just for fun. Instagram allows you to set up a profile page. You can have a link on your profile page, and what you are going to do is post a link to your landing page here. That way when people are curious after viewing your profile or some of your posts they will end up visiting your landing page. And this is all going to be free traffic and some of them are going to sign up for your email list. Once they have signed up you can then directly market to them.

Okay, so far we haven't talked about any paid advertising. And that isn't really the topic of this chapter but we are going to make a special exception for Instagram. The reason we are doing so is that this is not really advertising in the sense that most people are thinking about it.

Instagram is kind of a wild West unregulated environment. So what can happen is you can make trades with other people. There are two ways to approach this, one is a free way to do it, and you can also do it by actually paying someone. So let's take a look at how this will work.

For the first method, you want to find people in your niche that have a moderate amount of followers. They are also going to be interested in getting more followers and they may not want to spend a lot of money doing so. So you can contact them with an offer to make a trade. What you want to do in this case is to give a shout out and then have them give you a shout out in return. Basically what that means is that you can have them recommend to their followers that they follow you, and in exchange, you recommend to your followers that they fall this other account. This is probably not something you can do right out of the gate because you need to have some followers of your own. If you're trying to make a deal with other users that have larger accounts, in order to make it fair you can suggest that if they give you one shout out that you will put up three for them on your account.

Now let's look at the second way which is to actually pay to drive traffic. But like we said on Instagram this is not done in a formal way where you pay Instagram to run advertising campaigns. What you do here is you make deals with individual accounts. So you can contact people with large numbers of followers an offer to pay them to either give you a shout out or put a post up on your behalf. You might also be able to get people to temporarily link to your landing page. Or it could be possible to put the link in the post. So the way this is done is you need to contact them and ask them if they are interested in the promotion and what their charges are. Compared to most forms of advertising you are going to find that you are probably going to be able to get relatively low-cost deals that can help get you a lot of exposure. So for a mid-size account, you might be able to get someone to put up a post on your behalf for $35. It will cost more the larger the account is. We really can't give you specific numbers because everything is going to depend on the specific niche that you choose. But no matter how you look at it it's a very inexpensive way to get eyeballs onto your affiliate offers.

So that is Instagram in a nutshell. We recommend that you do more research into this topic and incorporate this exciting social media platform into your marketing efforts.

Email Marketing

One of the central components of any online business is having an email list. Before setting one up you need to sign up for a service each we discussed earlier. Then you're going to create a list for each niche. What we are going to do is create what's called an autoresponder. This is going to be a set of 5 to 10 or maybe 20 emails that are sent automatically on a schedule to people who sign up on your landing pages. So when they give their email address to submit the form they automatically start receiving these emails. In this book there's not enough space to discuss the technical details of setting it up, that is something that has to be researched elsewhere. What you need to know here is that this is going to be a vital part of all of your marketing efforts whether you are using paid advertising or free promotional methods.

The series of emails is going to be used too soft to sell your audience on your product that you're promoting. So you want to send people emails that contain useful information about the niche. For example, if we were marketing a ketogenic diet book, we could send recipes to our audience. Or we could send dieting tips. The point is you're going to email your list useful information and give it to them for free. The point of doing this is the same point of having the blog. You are going to want to be giving them lots of helpful content to create a bond of trust and establish yourself as an authority figure in the niche. You should also link back to your blog from the emails in case people haven't seen the blog.

Of course, in your emails, you are going to promote your affiliate offers but you want to do it in a casual fashion. Only very rarely do you want to do a hard-sell in the emails? So your first email should take a structure like the following. In the beginning, you start off talking about some specific problem or a set of problems that the people who signed up for your email list are likely having. If you have the same problem in the past that's all the better because you can give it an authentic discussion. But that's not strictly necessary, so you can do some research to find out what the pain points are for your audience. Think of your emails as short blog posts.

So it's going to fall to the same structure that we discussed earlier. What we want to do is after describing pain points that the audience have, they want you to explain to them ways to solve the problems. By giving them solutions in the emails you continue to build up trust.

Then toward the end of the email, you can state that you have found this product which really helps solve whatever problems you've been discussing. Remember that not everyone is going to buy the product immediately. So that's why we are going to send a series of emails, and you don't have to worry about doing a hard sell on the first email.

You can send emails about once a day as long as they have relevant content. Keep it friendly and informative tone. At the end of each email, you can recommend the affiliate offer. When you are recommending the offer include the affiliate link directly in the e-mail.

This is an old and surprisingly effective method of marketing. All online marketers or should I save virtually all online marketers use email marketing in some capacity. Practically every website you visit these days has a pop-up form to sign up for their email list. They are using exactly this procedure in order to drive client traffic. If you end up evolving to the point where you sell your own product, you are still going to use email marketing in order to capture leads and sell to them.

How many emails you want to set up is up to you. The point is to keep the emails useful and informative. As people buy it's common to shift them to the new email list. A list of previous buyers is more responsive and they may be open to new products in the same niche. So just as an example using the ketogenic diet if we were selling a product that was a guide on how to get started following the diet when people purchased it we could move them to a secondary list that sold them through a set of new emails a cookbook for the ketogenic diet. Or maybe it would be a dessert recipe book or something along those lines. The specifics aren't important we just want to you to see the way that you can tap customers to sell multiple affiliate offers in the same niche. Using these techniques someone who was initially a $27 sale might end up sending you hundreds of dollars over time.

4. How Affiliate Marketing is a money making machine

One of the easiest ways in which you can make money online is by engaging in affiliate marketing. You don't have to work on product ideas, product creation, providing customer support, or any other problems that are associated with the creation and development of a product. All that you need to do is promote a product.

Build Your Website Traffic First and be Patient

Affiliate marketing thrives on people's interest in clicking on links to products that catch their eye. But who are these "people"? All those who visit your blog or website to read what you have written. So, your blog or site must be as interesting as possible, if you are interested in luring them. Remember that you need to establish a good reader base in order to land an affiliate marketing gig. Your content must be as engaging as the look of your blog or website.

If you're not getting a good number of unique visitors to your website, then you're less likely to get the click-through to your affiliate. Here, "unique" refers to new customers and not the same old ones who have probably bookmarked you and keep visiting all the time. The traffic to your blog or site increases when the number of people visiting it increases. Not everyone is going to click on the links, and to get a reasonable number of clicks, you need plenty of regular visitors. You also need to build up a reputation as an expert in your niche before people will trust you enough to go for your recommendations. There must be interesting content for people to read and remain glued. It is not helpful if they visit just once and immediately forget about your blog. You need to track the number of people who visit your page and record the numbers per day, per month, and per year. This will help you to know how popular your blog really is.

One Good Product or Business is enough

Now that we understand who these "people" are who will ensure good traffic comes your way, let us look at what they will be interested in.

Newcomers to the system often make the mistake of peppering their site or sites with lots of different things, imagining that people are likely to buy more because they have more choices. It is typical human thinking to want a number of choices in anything and everything, let alone links on a website. You are not a store – you don't have to offer your customers choices, because they did not land on your site with a purchase in mind. They're there for information, and if you're good at what you do, you'll be able to persuade them to buy something while they are there, so you can make some cash.

Think of it as a classy gig to have only one website promotion and that website is the best one that your readers can have. That is, you will be able to promote one product or service better rather than having to do it for five or six different ones. Not only will that confuse your customers, but it will confuse you as well. You will have to look into two or three different companies and think of where their links will look the best. Think of yourself as a pop-up store to promote one product as opposed to a supermarket that offers a lot of choices.

The power of suggestion works on a majority of the customers. They will take a liking to something if you tell them that you are offering them the same product that you have personally tested and liked yourself.

Don't make the mistake of putting up too many choices at once. If you have put up just one product and the website is offering it at the best price in the market, then even if the person has left your site to do a quick price comparison, he or she is sure to return to yours to click on the ad. Also, focusing on a single product or business makes it easier to make keywords work for you. So, stick with one business or product. If you want to do more, set up a different website for each affiliate, and concentrate on that, rather than spreading yourself too thinly. What you can then do is link your sites.

Content is Very Important

This is true of any website, of course, but it's especially relevant if you are hoping to make money from affiliate marketing. People go to websites to be informed or entertained – often both at the same time. So, make sure you have plenty of content structured around the products or business you are promoting.

Another point to remember is that search engines can tell whether there's quality content on your site and will rank it higher as a result. That means more visitors and hopefully more sales. You must be well versed with the concept of "SEO." SEO refers to search engine optimization. You must have heard that many companies have a good SEO team that helps them become popular. Well, this is true because these teams will work hard on promoting the websites and blogs of the company and help it appear at the top of the Google search list.

You must pick out all the top words from your blog or website, that are most likely going to be typed by people. If they get the combination of words right, then your site is going to appear as the topmost links. For this, you can also make use of a small description that will help you put in all the main words.

But remember just a good SEO description will not do the trick and you need to have good content as well. So, forget about the keyword-stuffed sales pitches when you are coming up with content for your blog – educate, inform, entertain, but whatever you do, don't spam. You don't need long articles – in fact, three hundred-word posts will hold the attention of your audience better than one 800 to 900-word post. The more information you give away, the better the reader base. Most people will look for sites that give them an in-depth look at difficult topics. By making it easy for them, you will have the opportunity to increase your reader base.

You need to be as different and unique as possible. For instance, if you wish to provide customers with recipe ideas then come up with good and unique ones that are not easily available on the Internet. Once they take a liking to your unique recipes, they will be interested in clicking on an ad in your site, which might be a particular cream cheese brand, or even baking trays. You can also explicitly mention that you have used these brands and hyperlink the products with the words. Your readers are sure to click on them!

Keep the posts on the topic and plant the idea in the reader's mind that they need to buy whatever you're promoting. You can even drop a contextual link to a particular product. Help them reach a decision, rather than trying to direct them straight to the sales site. The soft approach is the best approach here as you are trying to be subtle about your promoting. I am sure you yourself have bought many things by clicking on ads put up on blogs and sites that you read.

Promote Your Site

This sounds obvious, but if you want people to come to your site, read your content, and click on your affiliate links, you need to let them know the site exists. Whether it is a product or a service, everything needs to be promoted for people to be aware of what you are doing. Without proper promotion, how are you going to get word about your website out there? There are only so many friends that will click on your links, and in order for you to land a big gig, you will need at least 1000 clicks a week.

Firstly, list your site in search engines, write press releases to be distributed online, and promote your site on forums in your niche and social media.

If you have a friend whose blog is extremely popular then you can consider asking him or her to subtly promote yours on theirs. But you might have to consider paying them a small fee for it, as you will be benefitting from their service to you. If you don't have any such friends, but know of someone who has such a blog, then you can consider contacting them and asking them politely to promote yours. It's a good idea to have Facebook and Twitter accounts linked to your website and set up so that each time you post an update on the site it's posted to your social media account. You can also have a Facebook page dedicated to your website or blog where you will keep updating links to your site. Work on building an army of followers, but don't ever consider buying them. Bought followers are not going to go to your website and click on the affiliate links – they just give a false illusion that your social media account is more popular than it really is. You might think of being popular, but once the bubble bursts, you might be extremely disappointed. If it is a group of friends, then make sure the group is genuinely interested in your blog or site and are not doing you a favor. Those will only last for a while and decide to abandon you once they lose interest.

Don't be Invisible or Anonymous

This is a golden rule. First and foremost, you have to have confidence in who you are and what you do. If you don't have self-confidence, then it will not work in your favor. Just because it's easy to hide behind an alias on the Internet, it doesn't mean you should. It can be tempting to use a cool name but don't do it. If you want to build credibility and earn money online, you have to be seen as a real person, with proper contact details. Don't hide behind a pen name or a nickname, use a real name and an email address tied to your domain name, rather than a Hotmail or an AOL account. If you wish to use a pen name, then consider putting it in brackets so that the person is aware of your real name as well. Make sure you write out your full name including initials, as there can be many others with the same name as you. Remember that people need to know they can contact you with questions and that they will get an answer from a real person. They might also ask for a genuine photograph, just to be sure of who the other person is. If they can't trust the Webmaster, they're not going to click on the affiliate link, and you won't make any money. It's all about trustworthiness.

Before you start to make money from affiliate marketing, you need to have your site set up to encourage people to click through on the advertising links. That means having great content that's informative and/or entertaining, earning a reputation for being an expert in your niche and taking a soft approach to selling. Let your knowledge and enthusiasm persuade the reader to click through, rather than filling the site with banners and sales pitches. Also, be sure to provide proper contact details so your readers know you are a real person. Now you're ready to sell, but what are the best affiliate products to sell, and how can you get started?

5.   Build A Website

Are you in doubt about the need to create your own website for affiliate marketing?

There are various ways to make money as an internet marketer without owning a website. You must have met or seen people who make millions networking on Facebook and Google. That's not bad but then is there anything that stops you from owning a web? Nothing beats having your own virtual estate, the value in the long run is usually profound.

More so, unlike the other networking platforms, you are in charge of your own website. Anything could happen to a Facebook account. What if after years of growing your FB fan page, the system brought up some modifications that brought an end to your page? Is it that easy to start all over?

You will be doing yourself a great favor creating your own website. At least, it is certain that your affiliate marketing can enjoy continuity and longevity.

Easy Ways to Choose your Website Niche Topic

Here, you will be guided on how to build your own website or blog. Even if you own a blog already, don't stop reading. You also have a lot to learn and unlearn. Are you ready?

1. Figure out your interests.

Interest is very important. So, don't be offended that I'm repeating this. Make sure you build a website that speaks volume of self, and your drive about what you want to share with web visitors. Ensure it is not something you will one day wake up and be bored about. You will definitely spend a great deal of effort reviewing and recommending products, and it is easier when it aligns with your knowledge and taste.

2. Narrow the topic.

You can't appeal to every angle of the market. It is best you narrow down the topic for your website. Then, you can have categories without losing your focus.

3. Conduct adequate research on your topic of choice.

With research comes clarity. It gives a clearer perspective on your targets, and the products you wish to talk about on your website. Don't hesitate to visit Amazon.com for more insights. You will be marketing their products after all.

4. Use main keyword in your URL or domain name.

Having decided on your niche topic, make sure you include the best keyword in your URL or domain name. There is something about the name of your website or blog that says something about its focus. Don't forget that! Don't forget to use that which web users are more likely to make a search on. For a weight loss niche, a URL like *www.weightloss.com* is better than *www.johnsmithblog.com*. Being specific will help to raise your ranking when people search for related keyword on Google.

5. Learn some basic formatting.

You have a lot to learn before the job and on the job. You need to know how to insert images, use hyperlinks, and other elementary formatting skills. Some of the website hosting platforms are surely easy to use and you'll understand more functions as you become familiar with them.

6. Choose a theme.

Consider the kind of theme that showcases the website's goal. Also, it should attract the visitors. It shouldn't be scary though. If they don't feel at home on your website, they will definitely go elsewhere. But if you want them to stay and even discuss you with friends, serve them the best theme.

From the beginning of things, be certain about the theme you want for your website. That's even before you start creating your website.

It is even easier now because web hosting platforms like WordPress have you covered with ready-made templates. So, you don't have to spend time designing, you can pick any.

What Different Web Hosting Services Are Available?

At this point, you should pick your web hosting service provider in order to begin with creating your own website.

Below are 2 hosting services you can choose from:

Free hosting

If you cannot afford to pay, you can use *Blogger*, *Weebly* and *WordPress* to build your website for free major features. Although the website is free, some of them cut their fee in the future once you start earning on them. Let's say about 50%.

However, don't start on these hosting platforms if you have a future goal to buy your own domain. If for example, you have an article on a free website titled *www.weightloss.-wordpress.com/example* and also ranks as number one in Google search. Should you decide to migrate your website to a private domain, your link to that article will change to *www.weightloss.com/example* and ranking is likely to be affected.

Have you noticed that most bloggers prefer Wordpress to any other? Find the reasons below:

- Has various layouts and free themes.
- Writing blog posts and attaching pictures are easy.
- It features comment and sharing tools.
- Enables categorization of posts.

While any kind of free hosting website allows you to have a sub-domain in the manner of, for example, *yourwebsitename.wordpress.com,* it is not professionally advisable for a website that's for online business.

So, how do you build a free blog using WordPress?

#1: Sign up

Visit *www.wordpress.com* in order to start your free website. Prepare your email address, your preferred URL or name, desired username and password. With these, you can fill in the required details.

#2: Check your email

Following the above, you will be sent a mail by the system. In the mail, you will be sent a link to activate your account. Activation is your key to finalizing your registration. Make sure you activate your account in not less than 2 days.

#3: Sign in to Wordpress.com

Once you are done with registration, go to *www.wordpress.com* to find your ready-to-use website. Click on settings on your dashboard to put things in place as you want them.

#4: Design your website

On the same dashboard, use the application management features to set up your blog. There are FREE THEMES to choose for in the library in relation to your niche.

Also, you can type the name and tagline of your blog to appear in the headline when visitors view your site. This can be done on your dashboard under *Settings>General Settings*.

To enhance effective design and functioning of your blog, you should add widgets in *Appearance>Widgets*. Common ones are Categories, Archives, Email subscription, and Facebook Like box. Once you have your picks, lay them out in a structured manner.

Below are YouTube video tutorials that can guide you on how to create your own website. Click on the title and link out.

YouTube Tutorials:
- How to Create Wordpress.com Blog for your Business
- Overview of WordPress Dashboard
- How to WordPress Themes

While having your website hosted on WordPress may cost nothing, it has its own disadvantages. Would you be okay with having ads run on your site by WordPress? If your answer is no, you need to pay about $30 annually. Most bloggers opt for premium account as a result.

In addition, there are some limits to being able to create a custom website when it's free than when it's a premium account.

If you will sign up at *www.wordpress.com*, make sure you read and understand the terms of service. And be reminded that any free web hosting platform is at liberty to bring down your website anytime they feel the need to. Be aware!

Paid hosting
A paid web hosting service has two types: Upgraded version plus a premium plan and Website created with a self-hosting provider.

1. Premium Plan website builder

If you have some budget to spare for a good website, this plan is available to you on hosting platforms like WordPress.

The same steps apply like in the free platform mentioned earlier. However, here, you will be paying about $99 to $299 every year to enjoy premium and business plan value plus opportunity to use custom designs. This kind of plan puts you in charge and that's a winning way. It also gives your website a professional outlook because you can choose a custom like *.com, .net, .org, .co, .me* website address.

Apart from its blog feature, you will enjoy the following premium features on Word-Press's Blog feature:

- Custom design

- VideoPress

- Direct Email or Chat Support

- Larger storage space for your works

As a beginner, this is a good option because you don't have to create a website from the scratch. The plan you pay for has in-built tools that make the hosting platform easy to use. What's more? If you are not sure about taking the plan yet, you can test the free 14-days trial available.

Now, let's talk about how you can how you can enjoy custom themes or plugins on your website using self-service WordPress.

2. Self-hosting service provider

Nothing beats being in charge. And if you truly desire to win as an online marketer, you should work towards having a self-hosted website.

What You are fully in charge of your blog.

- You have a server that connects remotely to the internet.

- You can cancel the plan if you are not satisfied.

- This is because there is a 90-day refund guarantee. are the benefits?

-

To be more specific, have you seen a site with a kind of URL like *www.websitename.com*? That's what I am talking about. A web address that you can freely customize. Meanwhile, this comes with a price. The domain costs about $7 to $13 monthly and approximately a total of $50 to $100 yearly.

I have however noticed that most bloggers would rather purchase domain and hosting from one source. This is not bad but you should ensure that you have a professional hand always available to attend to all maintenance needs of the website.

When you are ready, choosing a web hosting service provider won't pose a challenge. Just pay attention to the availability of WordPress plugins. Although most service providers have it, there is no harm in confirming. The availability or not influences visitors' experience on your site. Below is a careful guide to help you in getting a self-hosted website:

#1: Choose a Domain Name

Domain name is the URL keyword that you have decided to name your website. It is like registering a business name but here, you don't necessarily have to create a company. At least, not physically. Please note that you have to pay a stated sum every month to use the domain.

Why should an online business require domain name?

Earlier, I talked about professional look. Let me be clear again. If you want anyone to take your business more seriously, get a domain name for your website. It's simple.

It even makes things easier for you in a highly competitive yet unsafe digital space. Customers want to be sure that they are doing business with the right person. Let them see that first from your domain name.

You may want to ask what the big deal is. Note that a domain registrar, like an ocean, exists which contains titles of owned websites or domains. So, when you have one, you get the access key.

To register, you may seek the service of registrars like *GoDaddy*, *Namecheap*, *1&1 Internet*, and *Dotster*] or go through a web host. I'd advise that you do so directly rather than go through a web host. The reason is to ensure you are the one registered for the domain name.

To do this, make ready a credit card or *Paypal* account for payment. Once you pay and register, lay claim to the domain immediately. From then, it is your duty to protect the login details of the domain.

#2: Set a web host

It is a virtual world, your website needs its own space there. That's what web hosting service gets you.

You will find many web host service like *Bluehost*, *DreamHost*, *GoDaddy* or *HostGator* on the net. Most of them have the least requirement of WordPress so as to make it work. But then, make sure it has PHP, MySQL, and cPanel so as to enable easy installation of WordPress. Don't forget that a web host service costs $4 to $8 monthly.

With web host, you will access unrestricted storage and monthly data transfer. In addition, you will have webmail addresses, and easy installation of WordPress plugins.

#3: Install WordPress through web host

Having signed up using a web host, you are permitted to navigate on the cPanel where you will find an automatic installer or WordPress.

Really, you can do this without being a PRO but the choice is yours. If you can afford to pay a website designer, please go ahead.

#4: Sign in to WordPress

Sign in to configure the settings after successfully installing WordPress on the web host.

Link out below to a **YouTube Tutorial** on how to install your blog on paid web host.

- Easy Steps to Create and Host a Website with WordPress

At this point, you are set to design your website on the WordPress platform. Navigate to your dashboard once again to set up the design of your website.

Unlike the other, you can use backups and install custom themes with self-hosted website. With a self-hosted website, you can have backups and install custom themes. Even the maintenance which it requires can be worked on based on your decision. Remember that the reason you paid for it is to be in full control.

The process of building your website is summed up in the graphical illustration below:

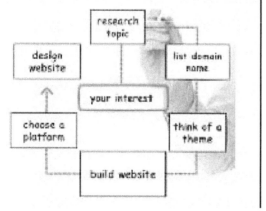

How can social media networks benefit your website build up?
You won't see how beneficial social media networks are to your website until you set up one. It is important if you want to enjoy more avenues to relate and share contents with

your readers. Most times, they are on social media networks. In fact, some live there. I mean it.

In addition, it is an avenue for you to improve your SEO ranking. Remember we talked about this earlier? Beyond just exchanging friendly chats, social media networks have grown as resourceful connections for business. Thus, it is part of marketing strategies.

The benefits are highlighted below:

- Opportunity to establish more links to your own website.

- Creates organic traffic.

- Unlimited numbers of social media users to market to.

Some of the social media networks that you can use to build up your website are Facebook page, Twitter, Google+ and Pinterest. Each has its spelt out benefits. See them below:

- **Facebook** – It is easier to find millions of users here among whom are those who relate with your market niche.

- **Twitter** – Although you can't say much here, you can also tweet about your business in few words. Use keywords that interest your targets. Don't forget to follow back when you are followed. That's not going to be hard as long as you make it clear from the start of things that your business has a human angle that they can relate with.

- **Google+** - Here, you can map out a group where people can follow you to get more info about your business website.

- **Pinterest** – Here is for images. When you are here, the words need to be out. And when the images you share are great, get ready for massive traffic. It's simple: Create a great post. Use high-ranking keywords. Link it to your Pinterest account. You are good to go!

Establishing social media account becomes easier when you have a theme for your website already. Mind you, your social media networks only support your website. They can't replace it.

It is also important to link your social media networks with the website. You can do this by signing up the same email address that is used for creating the website. Also, put the social media buttons on your website. How do you do that? See below:

1. Links directly to social media accounts on website.

It is common practice to have direct links on top or side of your web page. By clicking on the links, visitors will be led to your social media accounts.

There is a warning though: Avoid repetition. Avoid putting the same contents in your social media platforms on your website. As said earlier, social media only supports your website. So, the content there should be like additional information.

2. Share buttons

Share buttons allow you to enjoy the support of your readers for free. The buttons allow them to share your web content with their own social media contacts.

Managing many social media accounts for the growth of your website is really a tasking job. I'd suggest that you concentrate on one. That particular one on which most of your target customers are concentrated.

Also, this doesn't take much of your time as you can automate the process of sharing posts of on platforms like Twitter and Facebook via the Wordpress plugins. Besides that, you can always use dashboards, free or paid, like HootSuite Pro for controlling, scheduling, and interacting on social media.

What is important at this point, is picking your preferred social media account. Without doubt, most of the websites you see are linked to various social media accounts and if they aren't proven strategy to driving traffic, you won't see them on the increase.

However, don't make the mistake of purchasing likes and followers from your social media networks. Don't ever put your reputation in the line for nothing. Really, do your best and watch your website grow through the network of genuine targets.

Like building a house, foundation is key. When it is a solid and well-designed platform, your visitors will find you.

By solid foundation, let's be clear that what is being referred to is quality of content above quantity. After all, it is through quality content that Amazon special links will be included.

In years to come, whatever growth your website experiences would depend on how well you put the pieces of information contained in this book to good use.

6.   Promote Your Products

Is it now clear to you that affiliate marketing is about promoting a product? Hence, your complete success depends on how well you promote products on your website.

Obviously, it takes efforts and strategies to begin with affiliate marketing. Don't forget also that your website is a pathway for internet users who are searching for products to satisfy their tastes.

As a pathway, the motive of affiliate marketing is to promote products, not sell. So, make sure you create quality content that can help you do this.

How do you Promote Amazon Products Effectively?

There are important tips that you should be familiar with to promote Amazon products link effectively. Let's get on with them below:

1. Keep your blog active

Your website is the backbone of your online business, so it must contain valuable information as much as possible all the time. More so, consistent posting of quality content is important to SEO ranking. Even Google will testify that your website is active when you regularly post contents. Don't forget to focus on 'useful'.

Meanwhile, don't make the mistake of making your website focus on just one product. Else, visitors will view your website as being biased and overly focused on money-making.

Also, don't overcrowd your blog content with affiliate links. That's a big turn-off for your targets.

Still, you shouldn't rush into promoting too many products in a short period that you started. Even when you do, make sure you provide visitors with useful information if you don't want to suffer from lack of trusting and dedicated followers.

Trust and loyalty go hand-in-hand. And you must do all you can to establish them from the beginning of things. Where trust and loyalty are the bedrock, it becomes easier to make targets take whatever you say and whatever product you recommend on your blog.

2. Maintain only relevant products

When it is not relevant to your niche market, don't keep it. In fact, don't recommend it. Find products that are relatives to your niche, beat hard on how you found them useful hence, the recommendation.

3. Be honest with your reviews

Honesty is key. Online users are tired of lies. Be truthful about your experience with certain products. To share truthful experience about a product, you must have tried it too or asked someone who had. In doing so, you are recommending what you believe in.

Be in-depth. Keep it simple and interesting. Talk about how you came by the products, key features that anyone interested might want to look out for.

Establish subtle comparison in terms of price, pros, and cons. But let it balance so as not to be termed biased.

Conclude with tips and advice. This tells your readers that you are concerned about them beyond selling. Don't forget that you need to write in a way that keeps the buying mood of your readers alive.

With quality information, you will definitely get them hooked till the end. Good luck as you are on your way to becoming an expert in your chosen niche.

4. Use affiliate links regularly but don't overuse

Don't join the crowd by overusing affiliate links in your posts. At least not in the first paragraph of your review.

Only use two links in every post. One in the second paragraph and the second at the end. There is a greater tendency that the link at the end of the review will lead to conversion that the one in-between.

Also, ensure that the Amazon links have a no-follow attributes so as not to get penalized by Google. To do this, use: rel="nofollow".

To include the affiliate links in your blog contents, find a simple guide below.

- Sign in to your Amazon account.
- Find a product and search for "link to this page" text.
- You will be offered 3 options: (1) text and image (2) text only (3) image only.
- Highlight the HTML code and copy.

- Paste the code on your code.

The option you go for depends on what works best for your target. And know what works best for you, that's all.

Traditionally, people use different tags to evaluate which type of link generate sales on the blog. And when they create multiple affiliate tags, it becomes easy to track the links.

But based on comparison, people are more drawn towards a product when they are able to view image. Meanwhile, incorporating text link within the blog post is the commonest. Meanwhile, I'd warn you to avoid long product title in a text link. Keep it short. Two or three words are more than enough.

By the way, how do you build links on your website?

Have you heard about this WordPress plugin known as Easy Azon? This plugin makes it easy to include links. In addition, it allows you to search and add products (information and image) through WordPress dashboard.

Link out below to a YouTube video on how to insert Amazon Affiliate links into your blog posts.

- Learn How to Insert Amazon Affiliate Links into your Blog Posts

5. Use important keywords only

It is not enough to consistently publish on your blog. That you are promoting the right products is not even enough. The question is: Are you using the important keywords? This in itself requires a strategy if you want your content to meet SEO ranking. We talked about this earlier. If you want your website to be seen, use the right words.

All the efforts you have put into finding your niche come to play here, in promoting your Amazon products. And to make the best with promoting, you need to include important keywords in your posts. These keyword, in the long run, determine your traffic when online users make a search.

You don't just use keywords because that's what others are doing you. Keep it important- those that relate with your target market. Those they will use when searching the web. I won't stop reminding you of that.

Meanwhile, it must be stated that finding keywords could be consuming. So, I have listed below useful tools that you can employ in finding the right keywords for your target market. They are:

- **Google Ad words Keyword Planner** – This tool helps you to find new and common keywords. You should get ready because the volume of data it produces is enormous. You can also employ this in finding your niche market.

- **Yoast Suggests** – If you are looking for long tail keywords, this tool is for you. With it, you can expand on keywords that Google suggests.

- **Google Trends** - With Google trends, you can compare the traffic potential of various categories of keywords. This tool also puts into consideration demographics like the location of your targets.

These tools are going to be really helpful but you don't have to depend solely on them. You should also use internal search engine. You can always use Google Analytics to check the results of keywords on your list any time.

Don't forget that carrying out keyword research will guide you in creating contents that will better promote your products. Focus on getting the perfect keywords and you won't regret doing so.

By following each of these steps carefully, I will also add that you should take advantage of Amazon's widget. By installing them on your website, you will be able to put in more participatory feeling on ground for your web visitors. It's simple: When you add interactive features to the side bar of your website or even blog posts, it becomes easier to promote your products. Like never before, customer engagement is key.

Follow the steps below to learn how to select a widget from Amazon associates:

Step 1: Sign in to your Amazon Associates account.

Step 2: Right at the top angle of the homepage, click the "Widgets" tab. There will be a pop-up to let you in on available widgets such as Search, Carousel, and My Favorite.

Step 3: Pick the one you wish to add. Then, select "Add to your Web page."

Step 4: You have to configure the widget. To do this, fill out the details needed for the widget you selected. Be patient with the Slideshow Widget Screen, it may take some time to customize.

Don't forget to click and copy the HTML code displayed on the screen and then save.

Step 5: Open a new tab and go to your WordPress Dashboard. Open "Posts", select "Add New". Then add the Amazon widget to a blog post. At the top of the screen, select the HTML tab. Select the part of the post where you want your widget to appear. Then paste the widget code using "Ctrl-V."

On the other hand, if you will like to add the widget to the sidebar of the website, go to the "Appearance" section and select "Widgets." After then, drag the "Text" widget from the list to the widget section on the right side.

Step 6: To save or publish the widget, click "Publish" or "Save" button where applicable.

Below is a YouTube tutorial link to help you with adding an Amazon Associates widget. Enjoy!

- How to add Amazon Associates Widget

Tips on Blogging for Sales Maximization

At this point, you need to do all it takes to nurture your website. We have both come far studying rules and tips that will help you start as an affiliate marketer. It is important that you understand and follow the rules in promoting your website.

Yet, your success as an affiliate marketer doesn't start and end with merely following rules. More fulfilling yet difficult is the part where you have to promote products via your blogs and still ensure that your visitors feel 'at home'. It may be hard to make them feel at home from the onset. I however assure you that the moment they feel so, they will see you as one-stop shop where everything they need is catered for. Keep doing your best.

With dedicated effort, you will be surprised about how people who enjoyed great experience on your website will promote you through word-of-mouth. And really, what more can you ask of a loyal reader? Consequently, your level of income increases.

To effectively promote your blog and products, creativity is a big deal. Well, this is because it is not even easy promoting niche market. To help you on your journey, I have included useful content creation suggestions that can help you boost sales.

1. Include popular products.

Hold on, I have talked about the need for you to concentrate on your niche market. Let's break the rule here: You should take up monthly or quarterly opportunity to provide visitors with lists of popular products. This is not a small way to let them know you care. This doesn't mean you won't still keep your eyes on your niche.

2. Do seasonal content.

On special occasions, take your chance to recommend products that help pronounce the joy of the season. There are a lot of special occasions across geographical space apart from Christmas, Valentine's Day, and New Year. Seasons give you large opportunities to incorporate your Amazon products links.

3. Recommend bestselling products.

People are concerned and really want to know about bestselling products. They want to know what others are buying and would love to buy too. Isn't that summed up in the rule of camaraderie? Wanting to use or get what others are getting or so is not a bad idea, right? Don't deny them of such opportunity. And really, telling them about best-selling products in your blog posts won't prove difficult to market.

4. Grab promotional products that come with discounts and special offers.

Information is key. Constantly make enquiries and keep your ears to the ground on Amazon's special promotions. As long as they are related to your market niche, don't hesitate to grab them. And don't forget to tell your readers about the offers.

5. Encourage reviews and comments.

Mistakes made by most is to not leave room for readers' engagement. Let readers enjoy freedom to speak by giving their reviews and comments on your contents. It is a way of telling them that their voice matters. It reveals to them that there is a human side to your website. What does this say about you to new readers? "We are welcome here." And? They develop interest in trying the products you recommend. After all, another reader like them has said something about it. No one makes it in online business by shutting the targets out. Really!

Don't forget the need to build trust and loyalty. They are the ingredients that determine your conversion level. And how do you build trust and loyalty at no cost? Engage them on a regular basis with useful content. Wait, don't throw links to recommended products on their faces. That's not a good way to start. Let them enjoy useful contents.

I will like to remind you also that having a successful online business doesn't start and end with creating your website, writing product reviews, inculcating affiliate links, alongside widgets for Amazon products promotion. Beyond that, consistent effort and dedication are required in order to attract traffic to your online market.

While driving traffic to an online business engagement has proven effective, it has also proven difficult. But then, if you really really want to make it big in this digital space, be ready to compete with the leaders.

It is highly competitive in the digital space because driving traffic is an automatic exposure. Without traffic, no matter the aesthetic or the richness of the review, any website is as good as dead.

To increase traffic, you will need to engage the right strategies. So, let's get to know what you can do to be found by online users.

Highlighted below are easy steps to start generating traffic for your blog.

- Don't keep it from your families and acquaintances. They are your first loyal and trusted readers. Except, maybe, they choose otherwise.

- Include your email on your website.

- Learn to use some video creation tools.

- Create video and share the link via YouTube.

- Optimize your social media network(s).

Please, note the last highlight. It has been said earlier that social media networks are important to the success of your online business. If you don't have one already, now is the time. Purposively, use your social accounts to target audience. Keep the contents simple and attention grabbing. Don't forget to be interesting.

In addition, keep in mind the products selection processes and blogging tips I shared with you. You need them all in order to maximize your earning power as an affiliate marketer. Arm yourself with them and it will be easier to deal with any difficulty in your path to becoming an excellent affiliate.

7. Affiliate Marketing Tips To Make More Money

1. Get your affiliate site up and running with pre-existing material.

While affiliate marketing is a great way to make money online, it would be foolish to launch a new website and expect commissions to start immediately. People must believe that the items you propose are beneficial.

Don't tell anyone about your new affiliate website till it's finished. "The best-performing sites for us over the last two years have been those where we generated 20+ pieces of content before launching a website," says affiliate marketer Stacey MacNaught.

"It is easy to get caught up in how something looks," Stacey continues, "but we know that nobody will see the site until we get a certain volume of solid material up." "My own golden rule is to research and write out a huge list of content pieces ahead of time so that the site may launch with content in place."

2. Increase the number of affiliate partners you have.

Don't put all of your affiliate eggs in one basket to talk of diversity. A corporation can terminate an affiliate program, withhold payouts, or cut commission rates; however, this is uncommon.

(Take Amazon Associates, for example, which famously decreased commissions across all product categories.) Amazon affiliates pushing home improvement items saw their commissions drop from 8% to 3% with barely a week's notice.)

According to a good rule of thumb, no single associate partner should contribute more than 50% of your revenue. You won't be entirely broke if the worst happens. Replacing half of your income is easier than replacing all of it.

3. Take control of your audience's relationship with you.

Having a loyal, engaged audience who cares about what you have to say is vital to your success as an affiliate marketer if your content marketing techniques aren't reaching them.

Affiliate marketers that wish to spread their product recommendations usually start with social media and YouTube channels. Reliance on these internet channels, on the other hand, is risky for various reasons:

Many algorithms discount organic social media content to encourage advertisers to pay for advertising.

If your account is hacked, terminated, or reported, you will lose all of your followers.

Joining an email list can help you avoid this danger while also giving you a direct line of communication with your target audience. You have complete control over how and when your affiliate material is distributed to your audience, and you also land in an area where spam isn't a problem: their mailbox.

This affiliate marketing tip does not have to be difficult to implement. Simply include a pop-up window on your website that offers customers a free checklist or a discount voucher when they sign up for your newsletter (more on those later).

4. Become affiliates for things that your audience has recommended.

The audience of an affiliate marketer is certainly crucial to their success. Becoming an affiliate for the things your target audience recommends is a fantastic, under-utilized strategy to grow that audience while simultaneously generating passive cash.

Michael Keenan, the co-founder of Peak Freelance, did this with his freelance writing community. He noticed that members were looking for a new customer relationship management (CRM) solution, so he tested a few popular options. Bonsai won, and Michael joined their affiliate marketing program, earning money for recommending a tool that he already enjoyed and that his audience was looking for.

"As an affiliate marketer, keeping your ear to the ground is vital. Engage your audience in real dialogues. Help them overcome their reservations by experimenting with several choices themselves. Then join the best affiliate program and be compensated for assisting your audience."

Peak Freelance co-founder Michael Keenan

5. Know everything there is to know about what you're suggesting.

Unfortunately, affiliate marketing appears in practically every "get rich quick!" gimmick. This is accompanied by a slew of folks seeking to make fast cash rather than assist their audience. Those individuals have a propensity toward failing quickly.

"Having more expertise than your competition is one way to set yourself apart," says Mark Valderrama, CEO, and co-founder of Aquarium Store Depot. "You need to be recognized as an expert, or at the very least have a website where people can learn more about the products you're promoting to stand out as an affiliate."

"It's all too common for affiliates to pick a few providers they think their visitors will be interested in without researching them." Even if you're just interested in learning more about these topics, you'll want to know how and why others use them."

To do so, Mark advises that you "do your homework before signing up with a new service provider." Think about what other people have to say before trying it out for yourself, even if it's just the demo version." While driving sales for your affiliate products may take longer, when you do, people are more likely to trust the products you recommend.

6. Make affiliate links public.

Although honesty isn't strictly an affiliate marketing tip, it is something you should be aware of when recommending products in exchange for a commission.

Customers will not buy from people whose recommendations they do not believe. If you don't disclose that you're getting paid to mention a product, and they find out later, your credibility is shattered.

"Having worked with various affiliates in many sectors, the most important and finest piece of advice I can give is to be trustworthy. If anything doesn't appear (or feel!) right, your audience will usually avoid clicking on a link and may even avoid returning to your website. Repeat visitors, recommendations, and linkbacks to your site and overall business growth can all result from being trustworthy. You're forming a bond with your readers, and if you're not honest with them, they're not likely to return!"

Nancy Mai Harnett, Teamwork's Partner Marketing Specialist

It's not simply your audience's trust that you're putting in danger. The Federal Trade Commission (FTC) has strict rules to prevent affiliate marketers from deceiving customers with product endorsements. Any relationships with a retailer, including products you're paid to sell, must be disclosed.

For example, a disclaimer appears on Wirecutter's affiliate content. Anyone reading the article knows that the website will receive a commission if they purchase something through a link.

Wirecutter, for example, uses an affiliate link to drive traffic to its site.

7. Distribute coupon codes

As part of their program, merchants frequently compile a list of online marketing materials for their affiliates to use. The shortlist is usually made up of banner graphics and email marketing copy. However, it's not a bad idea to check with your affiliate partners to see if they have any active discount codes that can be used on the products you're promoting.

These coupon codes are also extremely effective at converting people who haven't tried your recommended products. If they could get a discount, 89% of millennial shoppers would try a new brand.

Once you've obtained a discount code to distribute to your audience, you can do so by:

I'm going to share it on social media with direct affiliate links to where you can buy it.

Sending your audience an email that directs them to the sale

Any affiliate-related website content that mentions the discount code should be updated.

To encourage searchers to click through, add "discount" to the meta description of your review pages.

For example, Sprocker Lovers has a product review for "Bella and Duke review." The availability of a discount code is communicated via the meta title as an incentive for people to click through and shop via the affiliate link.

Meta titles are an example of getting clicks from search engines so that shoppers can get discount codes.

8. Open an affiliate shop on Instagram.

To begin earning money as an affiliate, you don't need a website. New features are being rolled out by social media platforms, including Instagram, to help affiliate marketers get paid.

In June 2021, Instagram stated, "We'll start testing a native affiliate feature that will allow artists to find new goods available on checkout, share them with their followers, and earn commissions for the transactions they drive—all within the Instagram app."

Instagram affiliate shops are still in beta, but they should be available to eligible creators in the United States by the end of the year. Before that, focus on growing your audience. You'll have an existing audience to test your affiliate shop when it launches.

On Instagram, here's an example of affiliate marketing.

9. Create reviews and tutorials for products.

Did you know that nearly nine out of ten people read product reviews before buying something? You'll reach people already considering buying the item if you write reviews for affiliate products optimized for search engines.

Consider the following scenario: you're writing a review of Allbirds' running shoes. You use the target keyword "Allbirds shoe review," which 1,500 people search for every month.

You'll earn a commission on sales if people click your affiliate link, even if they were already interested in buying the product before knowing your site existed.

10. Make comparison pages available.

In a few ways, comparison pages differ from ordinary product reviews. They assess two solutions and assist customers in determining which is the best fit for their needs.

Users will be more likely to click your affiliate links if you publish comparison pages on your website. Optimize the page for the comparative keyword and guide users through the purchasing process to encourage them to click on your links.

The ClickFunnels vs. ConvertKit comparison by Khris Digital is a wonderful illustration. Both tools' links are monetized; the publisher receives a commission if a reader purchases either software. For both Khris Digital and the reader, it's a win-win situation.

A comparison page is an example of a page comparing two products to earn affiliate commissions.

Affiliate marketer Ryan Robinson uses a similar method to generate affiliate content. "I recently started writing a series of comparison articles that provide objective, side-by-side assessments of major hosting services to help users figure out which option is best for their goals and budget," he continues.

"While many of these hosting comparison articles have a low search volume (think less than 1,000 monthly searches), I decided to write a lot of them after putting myself in the shoes of a new blogger and conducting these comparison searches."

As an affiliate marketer, here's an example of how to make a versus page to persuade people to buy a product you've evaluated.

"I collect an affiliate commission on the back end whenever someone reads my comparison article, clicks a link, and decides to sign up with one of the providers I'm covering," Ryan explains.

"And the best part is that I'm an affiliate for both of the hosting companies I'm comparing, so regardless of which conclusion I recommend in one of these articles, I still have a chance to make a sale if a reader connects with something about the company I'm less enthusiastic about recommending." It's a win-win situation!"

11. Create product round-ups and share them on social media.

How do you tell if the product you're writing a review is worth your time? There's a chance your product review will fail, resulting in few affiliate sales and you wishing you'd chosen something else.

The Affiliate founder, Monica Lent, says, "One of the biggest mistakes I've seen new affiliate marketers make is writing long and in-depth product reviews for products that just don't convert." "The result is a lot of labor with little to show."

"Rather, affiliates should reverse the order in which they develop content. Create product roundups first (for example, 'best camera for travel') to see which products resonate with readers the most."

"Once you've determined which products are converting, separate them into dedicated reviews and link them internally as supporting content," Monica advises. "This method makes it easier to develop affiliate content, but it also helps [search engine optimization]."

This is a fantastic example of this in action. This Is Why I'm Broke publishes gift guides for almost anyone, including your parents, coworkers, and sisters-in-law. Anyone who buys an item recommended in the gift guide earns a commission for the publisher.

A product roundup via a gift guide is how affiliate links can be used to promote sales.

12. Think about the purpose of your quest.

The themes you should write about on your affiliate website are determined by keyword research.

Consider the intent of someone searching for that keyword in addition to monthly search volume and keyword competition. Is it their desire to be entertained? Are you looking for some information? Are you ready to make a purchase?

If you want to drive traffic—and eventually affiliate income—do your best to match affiliate content with that search intent.

"If they got the page by looking for 'best TVs' in Google, then they're likely close to make a purchase and expect to be swamped with amazing offers and suggestions, so you can be aggressive with your affiliate links," says Ted French, a search marketing expert.

"If someone looked up 'Samsung vs. LG TVs,' they might not be ready to buy just yet." You can still include a few affiliate links in the content. Still, your main goal should be to provide them with the information they're looking for—and possibly funneling them to one of your sales pages with affiliate links and recommendations if it makes sense!"

Jake Thomas, the founder of Golden Hearts, followed this method with his affiliate content. By typing "best for golden retriever" into the search field, he had Google's auto-suggest do the labor for him to discover new content ideas.

The phrase "best brushes for golden retrievers" was suggested first:

Use Google's autosuggest and autocomplete for prospective article ideas to get insights about search intent.

"I saw that all of the entries on the first page of Google were list posts, so I wrote a list post," Jake explains. "I added fear at the end of my title to help it stand out a little more because people like to know what to avoid: 'Best Brushes For Golden Retrievers (and Which Ones to Avoid).'"

"Finally, to make my essay more helpful and rank higher, I considered what inquiry the reader might have next," Jake continues. This resulted in detailed instruction on how to brush your dog, how often to brush your dog, and when to begin practicing with a puppy.

What's the result? Golden Hearts ranks first for "best brushes for golden retriever," a niche keyword Jake claims is "more likely to convert" because it "ranks for a very specific search and offers a specific solution."

13. Keep an eye on what's hot right now.

Buzzfeed has established a media empire mainly reliant on affiliate connections for revenue. BuzzFeed readers use the brand's content to inspire or support purchase decisions in seven out of ten cases. In 2019, the publisher made $500 million from this affiliate content.

"On all of that revenue, we get an affiliate commission—we make approximately a tenth of it in commission." It's a fantastic company with a lot of high-margin revenue that flows back to us. We could do so because we had such a large network and many people like BuzzFeed content. We spent a lot of time thinking about how people take action because we were focused on creating shareable content."

Buzzfeed's CEO, Jonah Peretti

Buzzfeed's affiliate marketing success is partly due to its focus on providing trending content. Its Facebook page regularly posts product round-ups relevant to what its audience is talking about, such as this list of inexpensive last-minute gifts.

Buzzfeed is an example of a company that uses affiliate marketing to make cash by covering product trends.

"Keep up with current trends and be open to new opportunities." To demonstrate your timeliness, replace that content with something new and popular."

RevenueGeeks co-founder Adam Wood

14. Provide a link to a landing page tailored to your location.

The benefit of having a successful affiliate marketing business is that you can reach customers worldwide if your partners distribute goods there. (This is especially likely if you're collaborating with Shopify stores.) International visitors account for more than a third of all Shopify traffic.)

Customers from all over the world have different needs that must be met during the purchasing process. Which is the most crucial? Prices in their currency, which most international shoppers (92%) require before purchasing from a multinational online store.

Link to localized landing pages to get around this. Many affiliate networks will do it for you right from your dashboard.

15. Place advertisements during busy purchasing seasons.

Your affiliate marketing business is still an internet business, even if you don't offer your products directly to customers. You get a commission on the products of another store, and the end goal is the same: to produce revenue.

Take cues from successful e-commerce marketing methods and time your affiliate promos to coincide with peak purchasing seasons like:

Valentine's Day is on February 14th this year.

Mother's Day and Father's Day are two of the most important days.

July 4th is a national holiday.

Cyber Monday and Black Friday (Awin and ShareASale affiliates earned $12 million in commissions over the weekend.)

Christmas and New Year's are two of the most festive times.

Invest some money on social media advertising, pay-per-click (PPC), or A/B testing during this time if you have the funds.

While customer acquisition costs rise during competitive periods, it's a wonderful method to increase your chances of growing an audience—your email list—when shoppers actively seek things to buy.

(Returning to our point about discount codes, numerous merchants provide coupons to commemorate these occasions.) Use them in your affiliate marketing initiatives throughout the holidays.)

16. Compile a conversion report for affiliate links.

How can you know if your affiliate marketing strategy products are selling?

Set reminders to monitor your most important numbers regularly, just like any other digital marketing campaign.

Clicks. A low click volume for a heavily promoted product could indicate that your target audience is uninterested in the goods.

The percentage of people who convert. The percentage of people that bought anything after clicking your affiliate link. The higher the number, the better.

Earned money. The amount of money you've made from selling a product.

The majority of this information may be found in Google Analytics. Affiliate networks and partners will have access to a dashboard that displays this data.

The purpose of reporting is to find out which goods are the most popular and profitable to keep advertising them and deprioritize those your audience isn't buying.

8. Affiliate Marketing Trends to Follow in the Present and Immediate Future

SEO

In this section, we will discuss SEO. If don't have the foggiest idea what SEO is, it refers to website streamlining? Basically, SEO is a method used to bring free traffic to your blog or site. It is one of the most ideal ways you can get more traffic to your website or blog. More traffic means more deals. That is dependably on or more when you are attempting to profit on the web.

It is said by a few, that there is no better way of getting traffic to your site than upgrading your SEO. However, beyond a doubt, paid advertisements will get you traffic significantly quicker than improving SEO. Regardless, it is essential that you service your SEO from the start. In this section, we will discuss strategies to consider so as to expand your SEO and get more traffic to your blog.

Having your site appear higher on the Google internet searcher is the way to progress. There are 3.5 billion searches done on Google on any given day. Which implies it would be absurd to neglect SEO development as you would leave a great deal on the table. Despite the fact that SEO can be an highly convoluted process to upgrade, we will make it simple for you in this section. We will go through the essential but best approaches you have to take for you to develop your blog and get more and more site visitors, which means more money in your pocket. All you will require is some additional time and persistence.

Backlinks

The most ideal approach to upgrade your site through SEO is through making backlinks. A backlink is the where you go on another blog identified with your niche and you add a connection to your site. There's a system on the best way to do it. A great many people are good; they can sniff out anybody trying to make backlinks. In the blogging scene, if you have a complex backlink, individuals can and will delete your connection, or surprisingly more dreadful, report you.

It is easy for you to do this procedure the correct way to yield the most ideal results. The best approach to make backlinks is rather direct. To begin with, go on different websites identified with your niche. Then leave a comment on their blogs composing a message saying "Hello, I really like your blog and I learned a lot from it. What's your opinion about this similar blog entry which I read?" Then add the link.

You need to prove that you're there to become familiar with their blog instead of developing your blog. Making backlinks will enable you to rank higher in SEO. The more links you have on different sites, the better the chances of Google positioning you higher up the web index. Likewise making backlinks is an great way to get free traffic to your blog, which is the most recognized way for individuals to get traffic.

Social offers

So, the next step for you to develop your SEO is get more and more social offers. Now the good news is, you don't have to get social offers from other individuals. You can do so by posting your blog in Facebook groups and comments associated with your niche. Now the main social sites to build on would be 1. Facebook 2. Twitter 3. Instagram 4. Google+. These are the top sites for you to get a huge amount of free traffic and to produce a better quality developed SEO.

Just like making backlinks, you have to ensure when you're posting on these social sites or networks, your objective is to help or educate the network, as opposed to developing your blog. It is also suggested that you post two or three different sites into your offer, so you don't seem as though you're trying to develop your blog or site.

In certain niches, some Facebook groups or networks could have more than millions in reach. This means it would be a good idea to develop your blog on their stage. As it was recently referenced previously, the more links your sites present on different sites the higher the chances of you developing your SEO.

Also remember, we will probably get much traffic to your blog as could be expected under the circumstances. Posting your blogs on the social sites and networks can enable you to create more traffic without spending a dime. However, on the other hand ensure you are a part of the network. Continuously review the comments section helping other individuals in the network, if you need a higher commitment rate when you post your site on the network or site.

Truth is developing your SEO can take years. Which implies you have to begin immediately for you streamline it to where you need it to be? Despite the fact that it may take you years to enhance you're SEO, that doesn't mean you will get no traffic for quite a long time.

The two techniques we just spoke about in this section will enable you to get free traffic from the earliest starting point and a great deal of it. You must be steady with it, which means making backlinks consistently for one hour and posting via web-based networking media platforms, etc. If you are original with it, you should have no issue getting traffic throughout each and every day. In the end, Google will observe your articles and streamline it dependent on how well your articles have been composed.

In all honesty, Google is great at discovering online journals which can have excellent content. You need great content over the long term. The more extended your site has been, the higher the chances of you appearing at the top of the Google web index dependent on the keyword. So, make sure to develop your blog entry from the starting point as you will be in a good position if you do as such, and remain consistent with it.

YouTube

A great many people don't trust me when I state this; however, YouTube is a standout amongst the most ideal approaches to get traffic to your blog. It is compelling to the point that we needed to make a section about YouTube. This is a great platform for you to advertise on as it gets around 30 million guests for every day.

YouTube is an expert with regards to promoting your site. So, in this section, we are going to discuss how to showcase your blog on YouTube. Likewise, taking advantage of this platform is essential. We will outline the best way to develop your YouTube channel to the point where you are getting a significant amount of traffic to your blog.

To make it clear, you don't need a million subscribers for you to see success in increasing visitors to your blog. You may utilize YouTube as a means to generate traffic to your primary source which would be your blog. For that, you are not required to turn into a YouTube superstar. Now, if you need to be a full-time YouTuber, go right ahead. Nevertheless, this isn't what we will show you in this section.

We will direct you on the best way to use YouTube to receive traffic to your blog. Depending on your niche, using explicit recordings can be expressive. I can't tell you how to make your recordings, since I have no clue what niche your blog is about. You may need to do that exploration independently. With that cleared up, let me tell you the best way to create more traffic from YouTube.

YouTube is a search engine

I have a question for you. If you need to learn a particular task where do you look? Your answer is YouTube or Google. After Google, YouTube is the most utilized web index on the web. For you to produce traffic to the site, you have to make recordings which are identified with your niche and provide information or help tackle an issue. For example, if your blog is in the health niche, you can make recordings on the best way to complete a squat or how to lessen lower back pain.

As should be clear, one video provides information and the next tackle an issue. You need to ensure that you are making recordings which provide information and help viewers tackle an issue. Along these lines, you can gain their trust, in the long run, getting them to visit your blog. The primary thing you have to do is make sense of all the current issues or questions individuals may have about your niche. Then make a video providing information and disclosing how to fix a specific issue.

The best part about YouTube is that it is totally focused on traffic. So, you will have no issue turning them into visitors to your blog. To improve this development, first, identify what your group of people is searching for. Second, give them the information they are seeking.

Getting viewers' data

You should ensure you are getting however many viewers' data as would be practical. In a perfect world, you need to get their email. If they follow your Facebook page and buy in to your channel, that would be an great start. Our essential objective, with the majority of our YouTube advertising, is to get viewers' emails. This will enable you to remain connected with the individual who is interested in your niche.

When you post another blog entry, the person who chose to enter their email will get a notice. Bringing more viewers to your blog immediately without you doing any leg work. Most bloggers drive traffic exclusively from their email list. Now there are numerous approaches to collecting emails. The most straightforward way is given them a gift.

Truth is everyone cherishes free stuff. For a lot of people, giving out their email for a bit of free information or guide would not be a major ordeal by any means. In the later parts, I will tell you the best way to make a sign in page for you to get emails. For the time being, I will examine the technique. What you need to do is after the end of your video, I need you to state something along the lines of "Hello if you need a free digital book on the best way to put on muscle, click the link below!" Once your viewers click the link, they will be prompted to enter the email to get that gift.

When you have learned how to collect their email, they will end up being a part of your mailing list. When you make another post on your blog, they will be informed through email and may turn into your most trusted group of viewers. These are the general population you need to offer affiliate products to. They will bring about earnings. All the more importantly, collecting email will be profitable.

Honestly, you don't have to infer any techniques on the best way to present your video to get numerous views. All you need is 1,000 views for each video, and you will get a lot of emails exclusively from that system. Our essential objective is to gather emails to bring in reads, which YouTube will assist you with immensely.

Ensure you are posting great content videos at least once per week, and in the long run this will make a swell of viewers allowing you to collect increasingly more emails as you continue posting. Just like your articles, your YouTube videos should be enlightening and all around detailed.

In addition, they should allow viewers to direct their questions. Likewise, refrain from running advertisements on your YouTube videos. You are using YouTube exclusively for traffic, not for money. Keeping your videos promotion free, you gain more viewers. Likewise, it will allow your viewers to stick around until the end of the video. This is fundamental for them to do, this is the where you will tell them you have a gift to offer.

9.   High ticket vs. low ticket offers

In affiliate marketing, you could promote high ticket offers, low ticket offers, or both. The choice of the type of offers or products you want to promote lies solely on you and your goals. A high ticket offer or product is simply one that costs more – consequently, the affiliate commission for selling such offers is often high. Low ticket offers, on the other hand, are those that cost less; hence, the affiliate commission you earn for selling them may be low as well.

For some high ticket offers, you could earn upwards of 80% of the cost of the product. So, depending on the cost of the product, you could earn as high as $1,000 for just promoting and selling one single product. Even if the affiliate commission for a high ticket offer is just 7% or 10%, you will stand a chance of earning high for selling the product.

For instance, if a product costs $1,000 and affiliates are paid up to 10% commission for selling the product, it then means that you stand a chance of earning up to $100 for selling just a single unit of the product. Now, multiply that by as many products as you are able to sell.

Most low ticket offers offer low payouts – typically the commission is usually hovering around 5% to 7%. For such low rates, you will have to sell as many products as possible in order to break even.

Now, one common question that most beginner affiliate marketers normally ask is, "what should I aim for between high ticket offers and low ticket offers?" There is no straightforward answer to that question as each of them has its peculiarities. We can also say that it depends on your goals and your marketing prowess.

For example, if you want to earn $100 in one day, which of the approaches below would you adopt?

Approach 1: Sell ten items to 10 people at $10 each
Approach 2: Sell four items to 4 people at $25 each
Typically, you would want to adopt the second approach because it makes your job easier. If you have the right strategies, it would be quite easier for you to convince four people to pay you $25 each for a product than it would be for you to get ten different people to pay you $10 each for the same product.

The final verdict is – it really depends on you – your goals, strategies, traffic sources, and the type of audience you want to target. With advancements in advertising systems, you can now target the right audiences as long as you know how to create a good ad campaign and a high converting sales funnel.

If you are going to use paid advertising methods to promote your affiliate offers, then high ticket products or offers are just the best bets for you. You don't want to spend a lot of money to promote a lot of products with low payouts instead of promoting a single one that could give you a higher payout.

Additionally, if you are using free traffic sources, then you could consider promoting several low ticket offers. You can also promote high ticket offers even if you use free traffic sources like blogs, YouTube, social media, etc.

Traffic sources for affiliate products

If you have the best or the most hot-selling affiliate product and you don't have a way of sending traffic to it, then your case is just like that of the person who doesn't have access to or know best selling products. This is to say that traffic is the lifeblood of affiliate marketing. Without traffic, no one is going to see the offers you are promoting.

Typically, there are two traffic sources – free traffic and paid traffic. Free traffic is often referred to as organic traffic while paid traffic is often referred to as inorganic traffic. In this section, we shall examine these two traffic sources and show you how to choose the best one for your business.

Just as the name implies, free traffic sources allow you to generate and send human traffic to a website, landing page or blog for free. It needs your commitment, time, and dedication – although all these could be equated to money, you are not paying cash directly for the traffic.

Popular free traffic sources include traffic gotten from social media pages, guest posting or blogging, YouTube channel, search engine results. Getting consistent traffic from free sources takes a lot of time and commitment. So, if you want to fast track your results, then you could consider paid traffic sources.

Paid traffic sources are those that charge you money to send human traffic to your affiliate offers, website, landing page, etc. Paid traffic can come from display ads, Facebook ads, Google ads, and a host of other forms of online advertising methods. Typically, most paid traffic systems use a PPC (Pay per Click) model to charge you for the traffic they send to your affiliate offer or landing page.

How the PPC model works is – you only pay when people have clicked on your ads. For instance, if you place an ad on Google and state your budget, Google is not going to charge you money unless people have clicked on your ads. This way, you are only paying money for the clicks received.

Now, most affiliate marketers make use of a combination of paid and free sources to drive traffic to their offers. No one traffic source is better than the other – it all depends on your goals, the types of products you want to promote, and your overall strategy.

That being said, before you choose the right traffic source, you need to make sure you have developed what is called a buyer persona.

Buyer persona

A buyer persona is simply a conceptual representation of your ideal customer. In other words, your buyer persona captures a mental image of who you think would be your ideal customer. In identifying your buyer persona, things you have to put into proper consideration include: what is a typical day in the life of this person like? What do they do when they wake up? Where do they hang out? Where do they get their essential needs? Where do they go to seek a solution?

You must identify your ideal customer before you go ahead to start sending traffic to your affiliate offers, especially if you are using paid traffic. Knowing your ideal customer will help you to know where and how to locate them. This way, when you are setting up ad campaigns, you would know how to set realistic metrics. Additionally, with a well-defined buyer persona, you will be able to choose complementary products that will be of help to your customers.

To capture or identify your buyer persona, here are a few essential questions you should ask yourself:

1. What is their demographic – what is the ideal age groupthat would need this product? Are they female or male? Do they have a family? Are they single? What is their average household income? Having answers to these questions will help you to fine-tune your research so that you could develop the right marketing campaigns that will get your audience to buy whatever it is you want to sell to them.

For instance, if you want to promote an affiliate product that teaches people how to make money online – typically, your ideal customer would include younger people from the age of 18 and up to 45 because they are the ones who understand the concept of online income. Your buyer persona would also consist of men and women. With all these pieces of information, you could go on your drawing table and craft out the best marketing strategy and traffic sources for the product you want to promote.

2. What does a typical day in the life of your ideal customer like? Normally, if you have studied the product you want to promote properly, you will be able to understand a few things about your ideal buyer. If you want to promote an inversion therapy table, for instance, then your typical buyer should be older people who have back pain is-

sues. Typically, most of them do not go out much; some are retired and may prefer Facebook to Instagram. With that information, you could choose Facebook advertising over other forms of online advertising.

Furthermore, you would want to find out the kind of jobs that your ideal customers have. Do they have a typical 9-5 job? What activities do they engage in before leaving home for work? What activities do they engage in when they get back from work? What type of TV shows do they watch? How much time do they spend in their car? Answering these questions will help you to determine who your ideal customer is so you can craft your marketing message to suit them.

3. What is the pain point of my ideal customer? This is arguably one of the most important questions you need to ask yourself when creating a buyer persona. Most customers will not buy the product you are marketing unless you prove that you understand their pain points. Normally, if you describe the problems of a person, they often get convinced that you could solve it.

If you don't understand the struggles that someone goes through, you will not be able to describe their problems succinctly to the point of convincing them to trust you. So, when you are developing a buyer persona, part of the questions you should ask yourself is, "what are the pain points of my ideal customer."

4. What are the goals of my ideal customer? Different customers have different goals, and you need to capture all of that so you can develop a perfect buyer persona. What does my ideal customer want to achieve? Do they want to lose weight, for instance? Do they want to maintain their weight? The primary reason why you need to ask this question is that you will need to incorporate your answer in your marketing messages to convince your potential customer.

5. Where do they go for information? Knowing where your ideal customer goes to for information will help you to know your best traffic source. Typically, the first port of call for most information or solution seekers is Google. This means that if you prioritize SEO (Search Engine Optimization) or Google PPC ads as your preferred traffic source, you will be getting a lot of traffic. Again, this depends on the type of product or service you are promoting.

Example: Let's assume that you want to promote weight loss supplements as an affiliate marketer. How do you define the best buyer persona for this product?

To solve the above exercise, we shall attempt to answer the five critical questions that are used to develop a perfect buyer persona.

Question 1: What is the demographic of your ideal customer? Normally, men and women alike tend to be bothered about their weight. However, women are always the ones most concerned about weight-related issues. So, if you are trying to promote weight loss supplements, women should be your ideal gender.

Furthermore, the age of your ideal customer should be between 18 and 60 years because that's the age gap that tends to worry about their weight the most.

Question 2: What does a typical day in the life of someone that needs a weight loss supplement look like? Normally, such a person starts their day by engaging in a few exercises. Some of them skip meals, especially breakfast, and they also go on different types of weight-loss diets. Some of them may have a typical 9-5 job and they mostly live sedentary lifestyles. They usually stay home in the evening, so if you are targeting your ads, you should consider setting it up such that it shows mostly in the evening hours.

Question 3: What is the pain point of the customer? For someone looking to lose weight, their major pain points include the stigma they face daily in a world where being overweight is synonymous with an abominable offense. Another pain point they could have is the issue of dealing with health challenges that are associated with being overweight.

Remember, this is just an example, and the pain points we have mentioned here are only for educational purposes. So, if you are trying to develop a buyer persona, you need to dig deeper and identify real issues that the buyer might be having

Question 4: What are the goals of my customers? Normally, the goal of someone trying to lose weight is to live a healthier life and perhaps get the chance to finally showcase that their perfect "beach body." So, you should include all of that when crafting your marketing message.

Question 5: Where do they go for information? People who might need weight loss supplements are those who are struggling with their weight. Typically, such people often seek information from those who have managed to put their weight in check. It is not uncommon for such an ideal customer to seek information or rather validation from Instagram, YouTube, or any of the other social media platforms. Sometimes, they might also resort to Google.

Now, with the above information, you can come up with a great buyer persona such that when you are crafting or creating your marketing messages, you will not have to do anything blindly, instead, you will be working with facts.

For the type of buyer that we have described in the above example, the best traffic sources for such buyers will include Facebook, YouTube, Google, and Instagram in no particular order.

10.   10 Most Common Mistakes

In this chapter, we are going to discuss the most common mistakes the new marketers make went taking up affiliate marketing. Mistakes can be costly of course, and one of the problems that happen is that people and up not getting the sales of their expecting because they been making mistakes, and then they end up giving up early. We hope that we can help you avoid this problem by 20 out some of these mistakes in the beginning so that you can avoid making them yourself. Many of us made these mistakes early in our affiliate marketing careers, so we pave the way for you so that you don't have to make the same mistakes.

Thinking people will just arrive at your website

We certainly hope that the readers of this book realize that if you just put up a website it's not going to get automatic traffic. Unfortunately one of the biggest mistakes that beginning affiliate marketers make is they assume that traffic just appears at websites. That is not the case at all. It might've been true in 1995, but these days there are so many websites on the Internet that's very hard to rank high in the search engines on virtually any keyword. You have to put the effort in order to obtain the kinds of rankings that you need in order to bring in traffic that leads to sales. So although there are our own preferences about how to get traffic, you've got to take want approach or the other. Or preferably use both. And that means you should set up your site in order to drive good quality, free, organic traffic. And then on top of that, you can advertise to drive more traffic. Simply expecting traffic to magically show up is not going to work.

Not providing enough content

One of the things about online marketing is that you have to have an inclination towards information. Just think about all the blogs and websites that you look at in your own browsing. Even though everyone says reading is dead, the truth is reading has simply moved onto the computer for the smartphone. People are actually reading more than ever. And one of the things about online marketing is that you need to be providing content to your users. If you're providing inadequate levels of content it's simply not going to work. There are multiple ways this can rear its ugly head in your business. The first is in your emails. It's easy to write emails that aren't long enough and don't provide the user with any benefit. Each time that you write an email you should be focused on one thing. First of all, try viewing the email from the perspective of the customer. Second, ask yourself if the email actually solves any problems that the customer might have. Every single time that you send any content out to prospects it needs to solve at least one problem that they have in the niche. Using our ketogenic diet example, one problem that people have is they get the so-called ketogenic flu. The details of this aren't important here, we are just using it to serve as an example. So if you were marketing a keto product our suggestion would be that you look up keto flu on YouTube, and on some blogs, and educate yourself about it. When you do this you're going to find a lot of suggestions from different people about how to solve it. So what she could do is write them up in an email. So you start the email out by stating the problem and in a compelling way. People on your email list that have experienced it are really going to resonate with that kind of content. Then later in the email, you provide the solutions that you found doing your research. And then after that, you suggested they buy the product that you are using in your affiliate marketing, mentioning that it really helps you get over your problems with the ketogenic diet.

So your emails have to be substantial and contain a lot of content. Secondly, and we already touched on this, your blog posts also need to have substantial content. Don't go and post three or four lines and call that a blog post. Remember what we said earlier, any post you put up on your blog should have at least 800 words. Secondly and this is very important and we should've mentioned this earlier, do not duplicate content. The search engines are not going to reward any website that duplicates content.

When it comes to YouTube, the same basic principle applies. A YouTube video doesn't need to be particularly long, but it does need to deliver something of value to the viewer.

Hard selling your audience

Hard selling your audience - we're constantly bombarding them with emails, isn't approach that Is doomed to failure. Often new affiliate marketers are anxious to get a sale and they mistakenly think that doing a lot of hard selling and pushing the product is what's going to result in a sale. Nothing could be further from the truth. As we stated over and over again and attempt to help you become an effective affiliate marketer, providing value to your customers is what's going to close sales. Bombarding them with emails saying buy this or by that is just going to turn them off. If you take that type of approach you might find that basically, you end up losing subscribers.

Too Many Products

The first mistake that people make usually comes about because they're anxious to make money. New affiliate marketers see all the products that they could possibly earn money from and they start imagining lots of income streams coming into their bank account. It's pretty easy to rationalize. If you start promoting 20 products, you might start thinking to yourself - well if each one only sells one copy a day, look how much money I'm making.

If there was one thing that you would've noticed from the chapter, is that it entails putting a lot of effort into promoting a single product. Or at the very least, what you want to be doing is promoting one niche at the most. That doesn't mean that you always have to promote just one niche, but when you're starting out putting up a lot of blog posts for most people is going to be pretty limited. You are simply not going to have the time required to be putting up with that kind of effort in three or four different areas at the same time.

Secondly, it can't be emphasized enough that you need to become an authority figure in your niche. It's not possible to become an authority figure if you're promoting multiple things at the same time. Don't get overconfident in your abilities and think that you can do it. Time and time again people have proven that taking on too many at once makes you unlikely to become successful.

It's understandable if you want to develop multiple income streams. And over time, that might be something that is possible. But your first task as a new affiliate marketer is to learn from scratch how to close sales. You shouldn't even be thinking about multiple products until you have a regular income from one product only. You can set a reasonable goal, maybe it's $500 a month, or better yet $1000 a month, and you will not add another product see your line until you have reached your goal. To be quite honest though, you can earn far more than that from most affiliate products. If you're doing affiliate marketing with click bank, that's doubly true. Of course, that's provided that you chose a good product, but there's no reason why you can't earn $10,000 dollars a month or more from a single affiliate product if you follow all the steps outlined in this book.

Not Enough Products

Yes, it sounds like we are contradicting the previous points. However, we're not going to be doing that. When we say not enough products, we are talking about for one niche only. So if we consider click bank as an example, you can find a product in some niche and sell it and make $30 from the customer. A lot of new affiliate marketers leave it at that. But that's a total mistake. You want to keep selling the customer. That doesn't mean continually pressuring them, but from time to time you want to offer them related products that you know they are going to be interested in. So if somebody's looking for weight loss products, new diet books, recipe books and so on. That way you can get more than one sale per customer and your $30 will turn into $100 or more.

Failing to Know Your Products

We have recommended that you get review copies of products you promote or even buy them using your affiliate link. That is something that you should see as an investment. It's an important investment because if you don't know the product that you're promoting, you're going to come across as shallow and unconvincing. You can't review a product that you haven't at least looked at. The more you know your product, the more authentic your reviews are going to be, and the more in-depth content that you can provide about the product. And this is one reason why promoting multiple products at once is not a strategy that is going to be effective. You simply can't know ten products as well as you can know a single product.

Falling Victim to Shiny Object Syndrome

One of the problems that come about when you're new to affiliate marketing is what we call shiny object syndrome. This is actually related to our first mistake that we outlined above. What happens is new affiliate marketers are constantly intriguing buy new products that they come across. Whenever they find something that appears new or is at least new to them, that new product makes the old product that they're trying to market now not look so good anymore. So they dropped the efforts on the first product and started promoting the new one. This keeps happening over And over again. So what happens is that the people never get around to putting in the full effort that's needed in order To actually drive sales from one specific product. You can think of it as having a bunch of half done projects lying around the garage if you're in the home improvement. It's far better to have one and only one product that you are promoting and driving to make actual sales and then improving on your sales figures, then it is to have five or six things going at once.

Spending money when you don't have to

It's human nature to want to take the easy road to matter what you're doing. And one of the ways that the easy road appears when it comes to affiliate marketing is that you can simply pay your way to success. People have a vision of simply setting up a landing page and then driving traffic to it which automatically converts into sales. We hate to break it to you, but that's not really something that happens a lot often. More likely than not you are going to make very good customers out of that kind of scenario. In that case, people will feel like they're just getting sold to. It's a totally different feeling if you establish yourself as an expert in the niche.

But the important thing here is that people get anxious in lower looking for an easy way to start driving traffic. People can up spending thousands of dollars on advertising campaigns that may or may not convert. When the fact is, you don't need to spend any money at all if you are patient. Just think about it what have you been doing up until now? You haven't been affiliate marketing. So why is it so essential that you start getting sales tomorrow when you can just put some time and now to set up a system which is going to dry free traffic from months and years to come?

So especially when it comes to people who are inexperienced, they start driving pay traffic and waste a ton of money. This might work for experience marketers because they will have a perfect email sequence to convert customers into the sales. But as a new marketer, you probably aren't going to be nearly as skilled. This means that your advertising campaigns are more likely going to be a waste of money. That is until you get your entire system set up. So, in the beginning, we really would like our students to put their focus on building a blog and learning how to write and write good copy.

Not putting in any time

Earlier we mentioned that people often make the excuse that they don't have time. If you don't have time why are you reading this book? The fact is there is no magic Genie that is going to appear and create an Internet business for you. Generating quality content and even coming up with good, effective advertising campaigns that convert is not something that you can just expect to happen – it only works out when you devote regular time to your business.

Failing to track campaigns effectively

At some point, you're going to be running paid advertising campaigns. When you do so, one of the most important aspects of your marketing and advertising efforts is to collect and analyze all the data that you can possibly look at in order to assess whether or not a campaign is effective or not. It's important to know the cost per acquisition of each customer. That is one of the most fundamental things you need to know about any business. Then you need to know the lifetime value of the customer. It's going to take some time to collect this data, and hopefully, you're refining your advertising campaigns so that they become more effective with time. But at each stage, you should be computing these numbers. So run your first Facebook ad campaign for a week, and then at the end that week gather up how much money you spent to acquire each customer, and then calculate how much money was earned from each customer. You might not even make any money the first week. But of course, we hope that you do. In any case, you might find out that you are either not converting enough from the Facebook ad itself, that is not enough people are signing up to your email list, or you might find out that your email list isn't converting. In the latter case that would mean that you need to refine your emails and write better ones. Over time, this is going to be a process of constant refinement. Also on the backend, without overloading customers, you want to be able to sell them multiple products so that the lifetime value of each customer is increased.

Focusing only on price

Another mistake that happens with new affiliate marketers is they see dollar signs when they find products that pay high commissions. That can be a mistake. A product might pay a high commission, but it might take far too many leads to generate a single sale. Ask yourself what's better. We could have one product that pays $30 a sale and gets six sales out of the hundred leads. Or we could have a product that pays $100 dollars per sale, but you only get one sale out of 400 leads. So you need to be comparing products across multiple dimensions. Simply focusing on price alone is extremely naïve.

Being cheap

Ironically, we are going to look at the opposite problem when compared to people who have been looking for the easy way out. Some people are actually too cheap. So what we mean by this? When we talk about taking the easy way out we are talking about people that think that they can only spend their way to riches, and they don't have to worry about providing content. At the opposite extreme are people that don't want to spend any money at all. We certainly encourage people to take advantage of every opportunity to use free tools. However, you don't want to be cutting corners by being too cheap either. One example of this is in choosing your blog theme. We touched on this earlier. It might be tempting to try and make a business out of its free website on blogger.com, or create your own website and use a free template instead of paying for one. But impressions are everything, and you need to spend money when it's appropriate. Saying that you're going to go entirely free could work, but it's not the best strategy. You have to be smart about spending your money, that's for sure, but don't try to save pennies when you're trying to build a business.

Failing to adjust the copy

Any affiliate marketers start out with extreme enthusiasm only to find that their advertising campaigns fail. Then they give up saying it just didn't work. That's a mistake, one of the things that you need to do is constantly test your advertising copy. Sometimes simple changes on your websites including your landing page, or in your text that you're your including in your advertising can't cause dramatic changes in conversion rates. Many times people will have an expert look at their ads or their landing page, and the expert will spot one minor mistake that was inhibiting conversion rates. You may not have access to an expert, but what you do have the capability of doing is A/B testing of everything that you do. So if you start running advertising campaigns and they don't convert all don't get all depressed about it. Revise and repeat. You can also look at changing images and videos. Have friends take a look at them and maybe one of your friends can spot something that you're missing. Often when you're too close to something it's hard to see something that's obvious to everyone else. A simple change of an image in an advertisement could suddenly drive sales.

Sticking to a bad product too long

In the vast majority of cases, the Affiliate marketers give up too easily. But sometimes people get emotionally attached to a product that they started to promote. They've tried promoting it using free methods and running lots of advertising campaigns, but they just can't seem to get a sale. But they keep holding on hoping that sales are coming around the corner. If you have run a reasonable number of advertising campaigns and you just can't close the sale you might find out that it's time to give up on that particular product. So rather than holding on trying to continue pushing a product, try finding a product in the same niche and then promote that one instead and see what happens.

Paying too much attention to gravity

For people who choose to be click bank marketers, which is a common approach for affiliate beginners, one of the mistakes that they make is they only focus on gravity. Now, remember that gravity is an indicator that gives you an idea of how many affiliates closed sales over the past 12 weeks. But that doesn't tell the whole story as we indicated earlier. Beginning affiliates often make the mistake of picking the highest gravity possible. And so then you have these newbie marketers out there trying to compete with two or 300 more affiliates selling the product. And many of those other affiliates are extremely experienced. They may have a huge Internet presence and be running lots of advertising campaigns. Meanwhile, the naïve affiliate who is just starting out might be ignoring a lot of Products that have lower gravity but the very quality websites that convert well. Of course, the only thing to do is to actually test. But combine analytical research into the traffic going to the website, the quality of the website, and other factors along with the gravity rather than just focusing on gravity alone.

Conclusion

Achieving success as an affiliate marketer is definitely not something that you can achieve overnight, and if anybody tells you that it is, they are telling you a lie. Affiliate marketing is certainly no 'get-rich-quick' scheme, however it can definitely make you rich if you're prepared to put in the effort and research required and make a commitment to building and developing a successful brand. A successful affiliate marketer will understand that there is much more to making money from promoting other people's products than simply setting up a website and displaying advertisements on it. In order to really excel and become the go-to site for customers looking to buy the kind of products and/or services that you promote, it's absolutely essential to build a strong brand image and reach out to your customers through a whole range of marketing tools, for example video, email and social media marketing as mentioned earlier. In this book, you've learned about the basics of affiliate marketing, how to choose an affiliate marketing niche, how to set up your affiliate website, how important it is to promote your website, various marketing channels used by affiliate marketers, how to build a strong brand and visual brand image, and how to consistently work at your project to ensure that you have an overall successful affiliate marketing site that is set to bring in a profit. Now, it's up to you to take all this information and use it to take the first steps towards becoming a successful affiliate marketer and eventually earning that passive income that you've always dreamed of. Whether you're considering marketing different niches like homes, furniture, electronics, online digital product, jewelry, or even gardening tools, the information in this book will help you build a successful site and brand to make sure that you achieve your business goals. No matter which niche you choose, the basic principles of affiliate marketing are the exact same and will work whether you're promoting products that are worth one dollar or one thousand dollars each. Whether you're a web guru or are just finding your feet when it comes to creating websites and using the internet to make money, it's possible to become successful and earn a good income from affiliate marketing.

Lightning Source UK Ltd.
Milton Keynes UK
UKHW032037090223
416755UK00013B/818